CONQUERING FEAR OF DEATH

BY LISTENING TO WHISPERS WITHIN

DR. MANMOHAN CHATURVEDI

This book is dedicated to the series of Spirituality seekers and philosophers

who have enriched the knowledge base of mankind

by selfless sharing of their deep insights

for benefit of the new entrants to this glorious path

Contents

Preface

Hari Om

My first exposure to death was when I was about four years old. It was in the native village of my mother, Bawal in Haryana, where she had gone to meet her parents along with my elder sister. My elder sister had medical issues and her condition deteriorated one night. Local doctor was called but she could not be saved.

As a child, I looked curiously at the contortions of sister's face as she experienced pain before her final journey.This narration I am able to make now, as an old man in his seventies. However, my recollection is that of a helpless observer, watching my mother grieve for her. The commotion in the household that just went around me left impressions that have lasted a lifetime.

In Lucknow, where my father was working for Indian Railways, my sister and I used to go to school together. I was a nursery student and on our return after losing her, life kept moving. Now, I used to go to school alone and I had taken charge of her toy doll, which I could never lay my hands on when she was alive.

As I grew up, many deaths in our family took place and I somehow registered them with sadness combined with helplessness.

Why am I talking of death? What is so special about my experiencing it, whether with emotion or nonchalantly?

There is some deep acceptance of death, though tinged with sadness, in my psyche and this I noticed during the death of my fellow officers in air accidents or otherwise, during my Indian Air Force service and more recently in the deaths of my parents and my younger brother.

Phenomenon of death has captured human imagination since time immemorial. All religions or philosophies try to speculate about it and also what lies beyond death.

I attempt a synthesis of the literature surrounding death and seek answers to the basic existential questions listed below:

"Is that all to life before we face certain death?"

"How do we face anxieties in worldly life when its fragility is continuously nagging our thoughts?"

"Why do all our worldly successes and pleasures emanating from them do not provide us lasting peace and happiness?"

These sets of questions are nothing new. Many before us have sought answers to them and all major religions and cults are born out of such endeavors by their founders. These questions touch on deep existential concerns that many people wrestle with. The finitude of life and the certainty of death can indeed feel daunting or even bleak when contemplating our existence.

Bhagavad Gita describes physical death in terms of an immortal soul changing a worn out body, in the same manner as we change our old or dirty clothes. However, this knowledge can make sense only after our body identification evolves to our true identity of an immortal soul through a direct subjective realization.

No amount of objective knowledge or reading Gita endlessly can take away our fear of death. Knowledge is important but only as a precursor to direct experience. This spiritual journey, may be completed in this life or may go on over several rebirths.

In epic Mahabharata, a story of King Parikshit and the Rishi's curse of his death by a snake bite is narrated. Fear of a certain death in seven days, made the King listen to holy Bhagwat Purana and acquire dispassion towards his physical death.

Listening to holy knowledge and its realization under the guidance of Shukha Mahamuni (Son of Ved Vyas) only changed his identification with gross body to his true Self, which is immortal. Of course, the King suffered a death from snake bite, as ordained by the curse of a Rishi. But, this was the death of an already dead gross body and his true self relinquished it and moved on.

If we realize that the true nature of our gross body is inert, without the association of our true immortal self, all fears pertaining to disease, old age and death seem to evaporate. Prince Siddhartha was moved by these sets of fears and on realizing the ultimate truth became Gautama Buddha, founder of Buddhism religion.

It is very important to understand the Advaita Vedanta concept of the phenomenal world as a superposition on the Brahman, the ultimate reality, by the example of our dream state. While dreaming, all characters of the dream are real to us. However, they are only superpositions in our mind which is the substratum on which a dream is played out.

On waking up from a dream, we realize the illusory nature of dream characters. Similarly for most of us the waking world is real, all characters and events are real, all our transactions are real. However, as we progress in the journey to realize our true nature and actually realize it beyond only intellectual conviction about it, we seem to wake up and realize the illusory nature of the phenomenal world.

A realized individual continues to interact in this world like the rest of us but his world view is changed. He takes care of his physical body like rest of us but to him other physical bodies are also equally important. He can not ever hurt any living being and is concerned about them equally.

In this stage of evolution, his physical body is nothing more than an outer sheath, a piece of cloth that he relinquishes without a whimper when ordained. Thus he has conquered fear of death and lives blissfully and so does die blissfully.

I am deeply conscious of the enormity of this venture and with all humility seek guidance from the ultimate source of this world around us. My intellect and experience is really insignificant and like a child on a sea shore, I play with waves to speculate depth of the sea beyond me.

In this book, we explore the issues connected with death by attempting a brief perspective using both oriental and western, religious and philosophical thoughts in chapters 1 to 4.

From chapter 5 onwards, we have attempted using authentic Hindu scriptures and through author's experience, formulation of an easy path for realization of ultimate truth that may help change our perspective about our physical death. Hinduism, one of the world's oldest religions, is a diverse family of traditions rather than a single, unified religion. We try to learn from Patanjali Yoga Sutras and Vedanta literature to guide us on this path. Three appendices at the end of the book may provide key concepts of Vedanta philosophy and bibliography may help those who would like to explore further in this vast domain of knowledge.

In compiling this book, I have extensively used internet resources and AI tools to help me organize the text on various facets of religious and philosophical thought. Thus an attempt is made to ensure that the Common Body of Knowledge (CBK) on related issues is mostly covered. My experience and insights helped me to validate and improve the contents further.

I hope this book succeeds in articulating the key issues with some perspective and people with similar questions and those seeking authentic answers find some value in it.

Hari Om

Manmohan Chaturvedi

About The Author

Dr. Manmohan Chaturvedi is an engineer by profession and holds a PhD. from IIT Delhi. He served the Indian Air Force for about 35 years and retired from the rank of Air Commodore. He had interest in Spirituality since college days and was formally initiated in meditation by Shri Vethathiri Maharishi in 1982.

Death has been an important phenomenon that has captured his imagination from childhood. Having lived a full life in the Indian Air Force, he is now attempting a short book synthesizing both Oriental and Western thoughts emanating from religion and philosophy on the subject of Death and how one could possibly deal with the fear that it creates in the human psyche.

He has been regularly contributing to a blog 'Search-within-Self' on topics connected with Spirituality.

Link to the blog 'Search within' is shared below:

https://search-within-self.blogspot.com/

Prologue

Hari Om

The fact that you are planning to read this book, claiming the possibility of '**conquering our fear of death through listening to whispers within**', may leave you a little skeptical about the practicality of this proposition. You are not alone. Spirituality and the endless possibilities that are projected about it leave most of us cold. Reason is our fear of the unknown. Spirituality sounds so esoteric to us.

It may be surprising to you, all of us are on a daily basis connecting with our inner self during deep sleep and have experienced the soothing effect that it leaves on us when we wake up. We have no memories of our meeting, no record of any whispers heard from within, as during deep sleep our recording instrument ie. the mind is also left behind in addition to our physical body.

However, without sleep ,we can not imagine continuing in this world for long even when most interesting things are happening around us. So this connection with our inner self is paramount and nature is taking care of it without our active participation.

Through this book we take you on a journey that has potential to connect us with our blissful self **while fully awake**. Few strange things happen when we move inward consciously. We experience murmurs within that are difficult to describe to others using words.

The experience takes place when our mind is stilled of all thoughts and is pure to reflect the inner self . It is like looking at the Moon reflection in still water of a lake. A turbulent or turbid water of a lake can not reflect the Moon clearly.

This journey has phases. For example, experiencing the exhilaration of a mountain top base camp is a necessity. Preparation for stilling our thoughts so that during meditation we may be able to view the 'Moon' of our true self, is essential. Preparation is required in all our other worldly pursuit too.

The good news is that our baby steps, following methods described in this book, can make it happen sooner than you realize it. All that is necessary is your commitment to this laudable goal. Pay-off is precious.

Happy Reading

SETTING THE CONTEXT

Hari Om

1. Introduction

Death, the cessation of life, has been a central preoccupation of human thought since time immemorial. It is a universal experience that transcends cultural, religious, and philosophical boundaries, yet its interpretation and significance vary dramatically across different belief systems and schools of thought. This chapter delves into the multifaceted understanding of death as conceived by major world religions and various philosophical traditions.

The concept of death touches upon some of the most fundamental questions of human existence: What happens after we die? Is there an afterlife? Does consciousness continue beyond physical death? How should we live in the face of our mortality? These questions have shaped religious doctrines, philosophical inquiries, and cultural practices throughout history.

In examining death through the lenses of diverse religions and philosophies, we gain insight not only into how different cultures cope with mortality but also into their broader worldviews, values, and understandings of the nature of existence itself. From the reincarnation beliefs of Hinduism and Buddhism to the heavenly afterlife of Abrahamic religions, the variety of approaches to death reflects the rich tapestry of human thought and experience.

2. Death in Major World Religions

We attempt to familiarise with central tenets of six major religions namely; Hinduism, Budhism, Judaism, Christianity, Islam and Sikhism.

a. Hinduism

Hinduism, one of the world's oldest religions, offers a complex and multifaceted understanding of death that is deeply intertwined with its concepts of the soul, karma, and the cycle of rebirth.

Central Concepts:

- Atman: The eternal, unchanging self or soul
- Brahman: The ultimate reality or universal soul
- Karma: The law of cause and effect governing moral behavior and its consequences
- Samsara: The cycle of death and rebirth
- Moksha: Liberation from the cycle of rebirth

In Hinduism, death is not viewed as the end of existence but as a transition within the ongoing cycle of birth, death, and rebirth known as samsara. The physical body is seen as a temporary vessel for the atman, which is believed to be eternal and indestructible. As stated in the Bhagavad Gita (2:20):

"For the soul there is neither birth nor death at any time. He has not come into being, does not come into being, and will not come into being. He is unborn, eternal, ever-existing, and primeval. He is not slain when the body is slain."

The process of death and rebirth is governed by karma, the accumulated effects of a person's actions in this and previous lives. Good karma leads to a more favorable rebirth, while bad karma results in a less favorable one. The ultimate goal in Hinduism is to break free from this cycle and achieve moksha, a state of liberation where the individual soul (atman) realizes its unity with the universal soul (Brahman).

Contemporary Interpretations:

Modern Hindu thinkers have reinterpreted traditional concepts of death and rebirth in light of contemporary scientific and philosophical ideas. For example, Swami Vivekananda emphasized the idea that reincarnation is not about the transmigration of a fixed soul but the continuity of consciousness evolving through different forms.

In conclusion, Hinduism offers a rich and nuanced understanding of death that emphasizes continuity rather than finality, personal responsibility through the concept of karma, and the ultimate goal of spiritual liberation. This view of death profoundly shapes Hindu attitudes towards life, morality, and the nature of existence itself.

b. Buddhism

Buddhism, which emerged in ancient India and spread across Asia, offers a distinct perspective on death that is closely tied to its core teachings on the nature of existence, suffering, and the path to enlightenment.

Central Concepts:
- Anatta: The doctrine of no-self or non-self
- Anicca: Impermanence of all things
- Dukkha: Suffering or unsatisfactoriness
- Karma: Intentional actions that influence future experiences
- Rebirth: The continuation of consciousness after death
- Nirvana: The state of liberation from suffering and the cycle of rebirth

In Buddhism, death is viewed as a natural part of the cycle of birth, death, and rebirth (samsara). However, unlike Hinduism, Buddhism does not posit an eternal, unchanging soul. Instead, it teaches anatta, the concept that there is no permanent, unchanging self. What we perceive as an individual is actually a constantly changing combination of physical and mental phenomena.

The Buddha taught that attachment to the idea of a permanent self is a primary cause of suffering. In the Sutta Nipata, he states

"As a flame blown out by the wind goes to rest and cannot be defined, so the wise man freed from individuality goes to rest and cannot be defined."

Death and Rebirth:

According to Buddhist teaching, at the moment of death, the consciousness leaves the body and, conditioned by karma, continues in a new form. This process is not the transmigration of a soul but rather the continuation of a stream of consciousness, like one candle lighting another.

The Tibetan Book of the Dead (Bardo Thodol) provides a detailed account of the stages of death and the intermediate state (bardo) between death and rebirth. It describes how the consciousness encounters various peaceful and wrathful deities, which are understood as projections of the mind.

c. Judaism

Judaism, one of the oldest monotheistic religions, offers a complex and evolving understanding of death that has been shaped by biblical texts, rabbinic interpretations, and historical experiences.

Central Concepts:

- Olam Ha-Ba: The World to Come
- Sheol: The shadowy underworld (in earlier texts)
- Gan Eden: Paradise or the Garden of Eden
- Gehinnom: A place of purification (often mistranslated as "Hell")
- Resurrection of the Dead: A fundamental belief in Jewish eschatology
- The Immortality of the Soul: A concept that gained prominence in later Jewish thought

Biblical and Early Rabbinic Views:

In early biblical texts, death is often portrayed as the end of existence, with the dead descending to Sheol, a shadowy underworld. The Psalms express this view:

"The dead do not praise the Lord, nor do any who go down into silence." (Psalm 115:17)

However, later biblical texts, particularly in the prophetic literature, begin to introduce ideas of resurrection and an afterlife. The Book of Daniel explicitly mentions resurrection:

"Multitudes who sleep in the dust of the earth will awake: some to everlasting life, others to shame and everlasting contempt." (Daniel 12:2)

Rabbinic Judaism, which developed after the destruction of the Second Temple in 70 CE, further elaborated on these concepts. The Mishnah, a foundational text of rabbinic Judaism, states:

"All Israel has a share in the World to Come." (Sanhedrin 10:1)

Medieval and Later Developments:

Medieval Jewish philosophers, influenced by Greek and Islamic thought, developed more sophisticated concepts of the afterlife. Maimonides, in his Thirteen Principles of Faith, included belief in the resurrection of the dead as a fundamental tenet of Judaism.

The concept of the immortality of the soul, distinct from bodily resurrection, gained prominence in this period. This idea was particularly emphasized in Jewish mystical traditions like Kabbalah.

d. Christianity

Christianity, emerging from Jewish roots and becoming one of the world's largest religions, presents a distinctive view of death deeply influenced by its central narrative of Jesus Christ's death and resurrection.

Central Concepts:

- Salvation: Deliverance from sin and its consequences
- Resurrection: The rising of the dead at the end of time
- Heaven: Eternal life in the presence of God
- Hell: Eternal separation from God
- Purgatory: A state of purification (in Catholic and some other traditions)
- The Second Coming: The return of Christ and final judgment

Biblical Foundations:

The Christian understanding of death is rooted in both Old and New Testament teachings. The New Testament, in particular, emphasizes death's connection to sin and its ultimate defeat through Christ. As the Apostle Paul writes:

"For the wages of sin is death, but the gift of God is eternal life in Christ Jesus our Lord." (Romans 6:23)

The resurrection of Jesus is central to Christian theology and shapes the Christian view of death. Paul argues:

"But Christ has indeed been raised from the dead, the firstfruits of those who have fallen asleep." (1 Corinthians 15:20)

This belief in resurrection extends to all believers, with the promise of bodily resurrection at the end of time.

Theological Developments:

Early Christian theologians, such as Augustine and Origen, developed complex theories about the nature of the soul, the intermediate state between death and resurrection, and the nature of the afterlife.

Medieval Christianity saw further elaboration of these concepts, including the development of the doctrine of purgatory in the Catholic tradition. Thomas Aquinas provided influential arguments for the immortality of the soul and the necessity of bodily resurrection.

The Protestant Reformation challenged some traditional views, particularly regarding purgatory and prayers for the dead. Reformers like Martin Luther emphasized salvation by faith alone and the immediate entrance of the saved into heaven at death.

e. Islam

Islam, the youngest of the three major Abrahamic religions, presents a comprehensive view of death that is intricately tied to its core beliefs about God (Allah), the purpose of life, and the Day of Judgment.

Central Concepts:

- Akhirah: The afterlife
- Barzakh: The intermediate state between death and resurrection
- Yawm al-Qiyamah: The Day of Resurrection and Judgment
- Jannah: Paradise
- Jahannam: Hell
- Qadr: Divine predestination

Quranic Teachings:

The Quran, Islam's holy book, frequently addresses the reality of death and the afterlife. It emphasizes that death is an inevitable part of Allah's plan:

"Every soul will taste death. Then to Us will you be returned." (Quran 29:57)

Islam teaches that the present life is a test and preparation for the eternal life to come. The Quran states:

"And We will surely test you with something of fear and hunger and a loss of wealth and lives and fruits, but give good tidings to the patient." (Quran 2:155)

The Dying Process and Immediate Aftermath:

Islamic tradition describes the process of death in detail. It is believed that the angel of death, Azrael, comes to take the soul. The righteous are said to experience this peacefully, while for the unrighteous, it can be distressing.

After death, the soul is believed to enter Barzakh, an intermediate state where it remains until the Day of Resurrection. Some hadith (sayings attributed to Prophet Muhammad) suggest that the deceased can hear the living and are questioned in the grave by angels about their faith and deeds.

Resurrection and Judgment:

A central tenet of Islamic eschatology is the belief in bodily resurrection on the Day of Judgment. On this day, all souls will be reunited with their bodies and judged by Allah based on their deeds in life. The Quran vividly describes this event:

"And the trumpet will be blown, and all who are in the heavens and all who are on the earth will fall dead, except whom Allah wills. Then it will be blown again, and at once they will be standing, looking on." (Quran 39:68)

After judgment, souls are destined for either Jannah (Paradise) or Jahannam (Hell). The descriptions of both in Islamic texts are vivid and detailed.

f. Sikhism

Sikhism, a monotheistic religion founded in the Punjab region of the Indian subcontinent in the 15th century, offers a unique perspective on death that combines elements from both Indian and Abrahamic traditions.

Central Concepts:

- Waheguru: The Divine, the Wondrous Guru
- Hukam: Divine Order or Will
- Karma and Dharma: The law of cause and effect and righteous living
- Mukti: Liberation from the cycle of birth and death
- Sach Khand: The Realm of Truth, the final spiritual plane

Sikh Teachings on Death:

In Sikhism, death is seen as a natural part of the Divine Order (Hukam). The Guru Granth Sahib, the holy scripture of Sikhism, teaches:

"What is born, must die; why lament what is inevitable?" (Guru Granth Sahib, p. 1244)

Sikhs believe in the immortality of the soul and its journey through multiple lives until it achieves union with Waheguru. However, unlike in Hinduism, the goal is not to escape the cycle of rebirth per se, but to live in harmony with the Divine Will and ultimately merge with it.

The Concept of "Good Death":

Sikhism emphasizes the importance of living a righteous life and maintaining faith in God, especially at the time of death. A "good death" in Sikh tradition is one where the individual departs while meditating on God's name. The Guru Granth Sahib states:

"One who dies while meditating on the Lord, lives forever." (Guru Granth Sahib, p. 142)

3.Philosophical Perspectives on Death

Philosophy has long grappled with questions surrounding death, its meaning, and its implications for how we should live our lives. Different philosophical traditions and individual thinkers have approached these questions in various ways. We take a look at major philosophical thoughts.

a. Indian philosophy and Hinduism

1. Upanishadic view:

The Upanishads, foundational texts of Hindu philosophy, view death as a transition rather than an end. They introduce the concept of "moksha" - liberation from the cycle of birth and death.

2. Bhagavad Gita:

Krishna teaches Arjuna that death is merely a change of bodies for the eternal soul (atman). The famous verse states: *"Just as a person casts off worn-out garments and puts on new ones, so does the embodied soul cast off worn-out bodies and enter new ones."*

3. Advaita Vedanta (Adi Shankara):

This non-dualistic school sees individual death as illusory. The ultimate reality (Brahman) is eternal and unchanging. What we perceive as death is just the end of a particular manifestation.

4. Buddhist perspective (Gautama Buddha):

While not strictly "Hindu," Buddha's teachings greatly influenced Indian thought. He saw death as part of the cycle of suffering (samsara) that one should seek to transcend through enlightenment.

5. Yoga philosophy (Patanjali):

Death is viewed as a natural process in the journey of the soul. The goal is to attain "kaivalya" or isolation of pure consciousness from matter, transcending death.

6. Samkhya philosophy:

This dualistic system sees death as the separation of consciousness (purusha) from matter (prakriti). True knowledge leads to this final separation and liberation.

7. Nyaya-Vaisheshika schools:

These schools view death more analytically, as the separation of the soul from the body. They discuss the nature of the soul and its journey after death.

8. Charvaka/Lokayata:

This materialist school is an outlier in Indian thought. They viewed death as the end of existence, denying an afterlife or reincarnation.

9. Jain perspective:

While not Hindu, Jainism shares common roots. It sees death as a transition, with the soul taking on new bodies based on its karma until it achieves liberation.

10. Puranic literature:

These texts often personify death as Yama, the god of death, and describe the soul's journey after death in vivid detail.

Now, we look at the views of Indian exponents on the issue of death

1. Adi Shankara (788-820 CE):

Shankara, the proponent of Advaita Vedanta, viewed death as illusory. He stated: *"Birth and death do not exist for the Self. These are mere appearances, like the snake appearing in a rope."* For Shankara, true understanding reveals that only Brahman (ultimate reality) exists, and individual death is part of maya (illusion).

2. Ramanuja (1017-1137 CE):

As the chief proponent of Vishishtadvaita, Ramanuja saw death as a transition. He believed that after death, the soul journeys to Vaikuntha (Vishnu's abode) if liberated, or takes rebirth based on karma if not. He emphasized bhakti (devotion) as a means to overcome the fear of death.

3. Madhva (1238-1317 CE):

Madhva, who founded the Dvaita school, viewed death as real but not final. He believed in eternal distinctions between souls, and saw death as a gateway to either liberation or continued rebirth, depending on one's karma and devotion.

4. Ramakrishna Paramahamsa (1836-1886):

Ramakrishna compared death to a man changing rooms: *"Death is like changing one room for another."* He emphasized that realization of God removes the fear of death.

5. Swami Vivekananda (1863-1902):

Vivekananda, influenced by Advaita Vedanta, stated: *"The whole secret of existence is to have no fear. Never fear what will become of you, depend on no one. Only the moment you reject all help are you freed."* He saw death as a transition and emphasized fearlessness in facing it.

6. Sri Aurobindo (1872-1950):

Aurobindo viewed death as part of the evolutionary process of consciousness. He believed that through spiritual evolution, humanity could overcome death: *"Man has to enlarge his consciousness, become a conscious soul, unite with the Divine and bring down the supramental consciousness to transform life and matter."*

7. S. Radhakrishnan (1888-1975):

Radhakrishnan, a philosopher and statesman, viewed death philosophically: *"Death is not a breaking off but a breaking through."* He emphasized that understanding the true nature of self removes the fear of death.

8. Jiddu Krishnamurti (1895-1986):

Though not strictly a traditional philosopher, Krishnamurti's views influenced many. He said: *"To understand death, you must live with it, invite it into your house, your daily existence."* He emphasized living fully in the present rather than fearing death.

9. Ramana Maharshi (1879-1950):

Ramana Maharshi encouraged self-inquiry to overcome the fear of death. He famously underwent a spontaneous death experience as a youth, which led to his enlightenment. He taught that realizing the self as beyond birth and death is true liberation.

10. B.K.S. Iyengar (1918-2014):

While known more for yoga, Iyengar's philosophical views on death are notable. He said: *"Death, like birth, is one of nature's gifts. But only if we know how to accept it."* He emphasized facing death with equanimity through yogic practices.

These philosophers, while differing in some aspects, generally view death as a transition rather than an end, emphasizing the eternal nature of the soul or consciousness. Many of them also stress the importance of spiritual practice or understanding to overcome the fear of death.

b. Western Philosophy:

Socrates (470-399 BCE):

Socrates, as portrayed in Plato's works, viewed death with equanimity. In the "Apology," he argues that death is either a dreamless sleep or a transition to another form of existence, neither of which should be feared. He famously stated:

"To fear death, gentlemen, is no other than to think oneself wise when one is not, to think one knows what one does not know."

Plato (428/427-348/347 BCE):

Plato, influenced by Socrates, saw death as the separation of the immortal soul from the mortal body. In the "Phaedo," he presents arguments for the immortality of the soul and suggests that philosophy itself is a preparation for death.

Epicurus (341-270 BCE):

Epicurus argued that death should not be feared because *"when we exist, death is not; and when death exists, we are not."* This perspective aims to free individuals from the anxiety of death.

c. Medieval Philosophy:

Augustine of Hippo (354-430 CE):

Augustine, integrating Christian theology with Neoplatonism, saw death as a consequence of sin but also as a potential gateway to eternal life with God.

Thomas Aquinas (1225-1274):

Aquinas, synthesizing Christian theology with Aristotelian philosophy, argued for the immortality of the soul and the eventual resurrection of the body.

d. Modern Philosophy:

René Descartes (1596-1650):

Descartes' dualism, which posited a fundamental distinction between mind and body, influenced subsequent philosophical discussions about death and the possibility of survival after bodily death.

David Hume (1711-1776):

Hume took a skeptical approach to the idea of immortality, arguing that the dissolution of thought likely accompanies the dissolution of the body.

Immanuel Kant (1724-1804):

Kant argued that belief in the immortality of the soul was a necessary postulate of practical reason, required for the realization of the highest good.

d. Contemporary Philosophy:

Martin Heidegger (1889-1976):

Heidegger saw death as giving meaning to life. In "Being and Time," he introduced the concept of "being-towards-death," arguing that confronting our mortality allows us to live authentically.

Jean-Paul Sartre (1905-1980):

Sartre, from an existentialist perspective, saw death as the ultimate absurdity that negates all human projects and meanings.

Thomas Nagel (1937-present):

Nagel has explored the "deprivation account" of death's badness, arguing that death is bad because it deprives us of future goods.

Derek Parfit (1942-2017):

Parfit's work on personal identity has implications for how we think about death and survival. He questioned whether personal identity is what matters in survival.

Key Philosophical Questions About Death:

1. **The Nature of Death**: What exactly happens when we die? Is death the end of existence or a transition?

2. **The Fear of Death**: Is it rational to fear death? How should we cope with our knowledge of mortality?

3. **The Meaning of Life in Light of Death**: Does death give meaning to life or rob it of meaning?

4. **Personal Identity and Survival**: What would it mean to survive death? How is this related to questions of personal identity?

5. **Ethical Implications**: How should the reality of death influence our ethical decisions and way of living?

6. **Mind-Body Problem**: How does our understanding of the relationship between mind and body influence our conception of death?

7. **Death and Time**: How does death relate to our experience and understanding of time?

Having seen the key tenets of six major religions and philosophical perspective both Indian and Western, in the next chapter we attempt consolidation of this knowledge.

CHAPTER TWO

WHAT ARE KEY UNIVERSAL THOUGHTS IN MAJOR RELIGIONS?

Hari Om

Part 1 : Introduction

The world's major religions, while diverse in their practices and specific beliefs, often share fundamental values and teachings that speak to the human condition and our search for meaning and purpose. This discourse will explore the universal messages found in Hinduism, Buddhism, Judaism, Christianity, Islam and Sikhism, with a focus on identifying the common threads that unite these traditions.

It's important to note that each of these religions is complex and multifaceted, with various denominations and schools of thought. We attempt to capture the core teachings and values that are generally accepted across different sects within each tradition.

Part 2 : Hinduism

Hinduism, one of the world's oldest religions, is a diverse family of traditions rather than a single, unified religion. Its universal messages include:

1. **Dharma**: The concept of cosmic order and individual duty. Dharma encourages adherents to live ethically and fulfill their responsibilities.

2. **Karma:** The law of cause and effect, teaching that our actions have consequences, both in this life and future lives.

3. **Reincarnation:** The belief in the cycle of rebirth, suggesting that the soul is eternal and undergoes multiple incarnations.

4. **Moksha:** The ultimate goal of liberation from the cycle of rebirth and union with the divine.

5. **Unity in Diversity:** The recognition of multiple paths to the divine, encapsulated in the saying *"Truth is one, paths are many"* (**Ekam Sat Vipra Bahudha Vadanti**).

6. **Ahimsa:** Non-violence towards all living beings.

7. **Atman and Brahman:** The concept that the individual soul (Atman) is ultimately one with the universal soul (Brahman).

Key texts in Hinduism include the Vedas, Upanishads, Bhagavad Gita, and various Puranas. The Bhagavad Gita, in particular, offers universal teachings on duty, devotion, and self-realization.

Universal message: *"The world is one family"* (**Vasudhaiva Kutumbakam**), emphasizing the interconnectedness of all beings and the importance of living in harmony with nature and each other.

Part 3 : Buddhism

Buddhism, founded by Siddhartha Gautama (the Buddha) in ancient India, offers a path to enlightenment and liberation from suffering. Its universal messages include:

1. **The Four Noble Truths:**
- The truth of suffering (dukkha)
- The truth of the cause of suffering (samudaya)
- The truth of the cessation of suffering (nirodha)
- The truth of the path leading to the cessation of suffering (magga)

2. **The Eightfold Path:** Right view, right resolve, right speech, right conduct, right livelihood, right effort, right mindfulness, and right concentration.

3. **Impermanence (Anicca):** The understanding that all phenomena are in constant flux.

4. **Non-self (Anatta):** The concept that there is no permanent, unchanging self.

5. **Compassion (Karuna) and Loving-kindness (Metta):** The cultivation of universal compassion for all beings.

6. **Mindfulness:** The practice of present-moment awareness.

7. **Interdependence:** The understanding that all phenomena arise in dependence upon other phenomena.

Key texts in Buddhism include the Tripitaka (Pali Canon) and various Mahayana sutras. The Dhammapada, a collection of sayings of the Buddha, offers concise teachings on ethics and wisdom.

Universal message: "May all beings be happy and free from suffering," encapsulating the Buddhist emphasis on universal compassion and the alleviation of suffering for all sentient beings.

Part 4 : Judaism

Judaism, one of the world's oldest monotheistic religions, emphasizes ethical monotheism and a covenant relationship with God. Its universal messages include:

1. **Ethical Monotheism:** The belief in one God who demands ethical behavior from humanity.

2. **Tikkun Olam:** The concept of "repairing the world," encouraging social justice and environmental stewardship.

3. **The Importance of Study and Education:** Valuing lifelong learning and the pursuit of wisdom.

4. **Chesed:** Loving-kindness and compassionate action towards others.

5. **Tzedakah:** The obligation to perform charitable acts and pursue justice.

6. **Shalom:** The pursuit of peace and wholeness in all aspects of life.

7. **The Sanctity of Human Life:** The belief that all humans are created in the image of God (B'tselem Elohim).

Key texts in Judaism include the Tanakh (Hebrew Bible) and the Talmud. The Ten Commandments and the teachings of the prophets offer fundamental ethical guidelines.

Universal message: "Love your neighbor as yourself" (Leviticus 19:18), emphasizing the importance of treating others with kindness and respect.

Part 5 : Christianity

Christianity, based on the life and teachings of Jesus Christ, emphasizes love, forgiveness and salvation. Its universal messages include:

1. **Love of God and Neighbor:** The greatest commandments as taught by Jesus.

2. **Forgiveness:** The importance of forgiving others and seeking forgiveness.

3. **Salvation through Faith:** The belief in redemption through faith in Jesus Christ.

4. **The Golden Rule:** *"Do unto others as you would have them do unto you."*

5. **Compassion for the Marginalized:** Jesus' emphasis on caring for the poor, sick, and outcast.

6. **The Kingdom of God:** The concept of a spiritual realm characterized by justice, peace and love.

7. **Stewardship:** The responsibility to care for God's creation.

Key texts in Christianity include the Bible, particularly the New Testament. The Sermon on the Mount (Matthew 5-7) offers a concise summary of Jesus' ethical teachings.

Universal message: *"For God so loved the world that he gave his one and only Son, that whoever believes in him shall not perish but have eternal life"* (John 3:16), emphasizing God's love for humanity and the offer of salvation.

Part 6 : Islam

Islam, founded on the teachings of the Prophet Muhammad, emphasizes submission to the will of Allah (God) and the unity of all creation. Its universal messages include:

1. **Tawhid:** The oneness and unity of Allah.

2. **Submission to Allah's Will:** Aligning one's life with divine guidance.

3. **The Five Pillars:** Shahada (declaration of faith), Salat (prayer), Zakat (charity), Sawm (fasting during Ramadan), and Hajj (pilgrimage to Mecca).

4. **Justice and Equality:** The emphasis on social justice and the equality of all believers before Allah.

5. **Compassion and Mercy:** The importance of showing compassion to all of Allah's creation.

6. **Knowledge and Education:** The value placed on seeking knowledge and understanding.

7. **Moderation:** The encouragement of a balanced approach to life.

Key texts in Islam include the Quran and the Hadith (sayings and actions of the Prophet Muhammad). The Quran's opening chapter, Al-Fatihah, offers a concise summary of Islamic beliefs.

Universal message: *"O mankind! We created you from a single (pair) of a male and a female, and made you into nations and tribes, that you may know each other"* (Quran 49:13), emphasizing the unity of humanity and the value of diversity.

Part 7 : Sikhism

Sikhism, founded by Guru Nanak in the Punjab region, emphasizes equality, service, and devotion to one God. Its universal messages include:

1. **Ik Onkar:** The belief in one universal God.

2. **Equality:** The rejection of caste, gender, and racial discrimination.

3. **Sewa:** Selfless service to humanity.

4. **Kirat Karni:** Earning an honest living.

5. **Vand Chakna:** Sharing with others and helping those in need.

6. **Nam Japna:** Meditation on God's name and attributes.

7. **The Oneness of Humanity:** The recognition of the divine light in all beings.

Key texts in Sikhism include the Guru Granth Sahib, the eternal Guru and holy scripture of the Sikhs. The Mool Mantar, the opening verse of the Guru Granth Sahib, encapsulates core Sikh beliefs.

Universal message: *"Recognize the human race as one"* (Guru Gobind Singh), emphasizing the fundamental equality and unity of all people.

Part 8 : Common Threads Among Major Religions

Despite their differences, these major religions share several common threads:

1. Belief in a Higher Power or Ultimate Reality: While conceptions vary, all these religions acknowledge a divine or transcendent dimension to existence.

2. Ethical Living: All emphasize the importance of moral conduct, often outlined in specific ethical guidelines or commandments.

3. Compassion and Love: The cultivation of compassion, kindness, and love towards others is a central theme in all these traditions.

4. Service to Others: Helping those in need and contributing positively to society are valued across these religions.

5. Self-Improvement and Spiritual Growth: All encourage followers to engage in practices that lead to personal and spiritual development.

6. Respect for Human Life: The sanctity and value of human life is affirmed in various ways across these traditions.

7. Justice and Equality: While expressed differently, there is a common thread of promoting fairness and equal treatment of all people.

8. Peace: The pursuit of inner peace and harmony in society is a shared aspiration.

9. Mindfulness and Presence: Many of these traditions emphasize the importance of being present and aware in one's daily life.

10. Interconnectedness: There is often recognition of the interconnected nature of all beings and phenomena.

Part 9: Universal Ethical Principles

Across these religions, we can identify several universal ethical principles:

1. The Golden Rule: Treating others as one would wish to be treated is a principle found in various forms across these traditions.

2. Non-Violence: The avoidance of harm to others is a shared ethical stance, though interpreted and applied differently.

3. Truthfulness: Honesty and integrity are valued across these religions.

4. Respect for Parents and Elders: Honoring one's parents and respecting elders is a common theme.

5. Charity and Generosity: Giving to those in need is encouraged in all these traditions.

6. Sexual Ethics: While specific teachings vary, all have guidelines regarding sexual behavior.

7. Respect for Property: Prohibitions against theft and respect for others' possessions are common.

8. Moderation: Avoiding excess and maintaining balance in life is a shared principle.

9. Forgiveness: The importance of forgiving others is emphasized in various ways.

10. Gratitude: Cultivating thankfulness for life and its blessings is a common theme.

Part 10: Shared Spiritual Practices

Despite differences in specific rituals, these religions often share similar types of spiritual practices:

1. Prayer and Meditation: Regular communication with the divine or cultivation of mindfulness.

2. Fasting: Periods of abstinence from food or certain activities for spiritual purposes.

3. Pilgrimage: Journeys to sacred sites or places of spiritual significance.

4. Communal Worship: Gathering together for religious services or ceremonies.

5. Charitable Acts: Giving to the poor or performing acts of service as a spiritual practice.

6. Study of Sacred Texts: Regular reading and contemplation of religious scriptures.

7. **Observance of Holy Days:** Celebration of significant religious events or seasons.

8. **Rites of Passage:** Ceremonies marking important life transitions (birth, coming of age, marriage, death).

9. **Devotional Practices:** Expressions of love and devotion to the divine through various means (song, dance, art).

10. **Ascetic Practices:** Periods of intentional simplicity or renunciation for spiritual growth.

Part 11: Approaches to the Divine

While conceptions of the divine or ultimate reality vary, there are some common approaches:

1. **Monotheism:** Belief in one God (Judaism, Christianity, Islam, Sikhism).

2. **Polytheism:** Recognition of multiple deities (some forms of Hinduism).

3. **Non-Theism:** Focus on spiritual principles rather than a personal deity (some forms of Buddhism).

4. **Pantheism/Panentheism:** Understanding of the divine as permeating all of reality (aspects of Hinduism and some mystical traditions in other religions).

5. **Transcendence and Immanence:** Many traditions recognize both the beyond-ness and within-ness of the divine.

Part 12: Concepts of Afterlife and Salvation

Views on what happens after death and how one achieves ultimate spiritual fulfillment vary, but often include:

1. **Heaven and Hell:** Belief in realms of reward or punishment after death (Christianity, Islam, some forms of Judaism).

2. **Reincarnation:** The cycle of rebirth based on karma (Hinduism, Buddhism, Sikhism).

3. **Nirvana:** Liberation from the cycle of rebirth (Buddhism).

4. **Moksha:** Liberation and union with the divine (Hinduism).

5. **Resurrection:** Belief in bodily resurrection at the end of time (Christianity, Islam, some forms of Judaism).

6. **Eternal Life:** Continuation of the soul or consciousness after death.

Part 13: Approaches to Suffering and Evil

All these religions grapple with the existence of suffering and evil, offering various perspectives:

1. **Karma and Rebirth:** Suffering as a result of past actions (Hinduism, Buddhism, Sikhism).

2. **Original Sin:** Suffering as a consequence of humanity's fall from grace (Christianity).

3. **Free Will:** Evil as a result of human choice (emphasized in various traditions).

4. **Divine Plan:** Suffering as part of a larger divine purpose (aspects of various traditions).

5. **Illusion:** Suffering as a result of misperception of reality (some schools of Hinduism and Buddhism).

6. **Test or Trial:** Suffering as a means of spiritual growth or testing (Islam, aspects of other traditions).

Part 14: Social and Ethical Teachings

These religions often have teachings that address social issues and promote ethical behavior in society:

1. **Social Justice:** Advocacy for fair treatment of all members of society.

2. **Environmental Stewardship:** Care for the natural world as a divine creation or interconnected system.

3. **Family Values:** Emphasis on the importance of family relationships and responsibilities.

4. **Community Responsibility:** The role of individuals in contributing to the well-being of their community.

5. **Economic Ethics:** Guidelines for ethical business practices and use of wealth.

6. **Peace-making:** Encouragement of conflict resolution and promotion of harmony.

7. **Education:** Valuing of knowledge and learning as means of individual and societal improvement.

Part 15: Conclusion

While each religion has its unique beliefs, practices, and cultural contexts, this exploration reveals significant common ground among the world's major faiths. The shared emphasis on ethical living, compassion, spiritual growth, and service to others provides a foundation for interfaith dialogue and cooperation.

These common threads suggest that despite theological differences, there is a universal human yearning for meaning, connection, and transcendence. The wisdom contained in these traditions offers valuable insights for addressing contemporary challenges, from personal ethics to global issues like social justice and environmental sustainability.

As we navigate an increasingly interconnected world, understanding and appreciating these shared values and teachings can foster greater empathy, respect, and cooperation among people of different faiths. While honoring the unique contributions of each tradition, recognizing our common humanity and shared spiritual aspirations can be a powerful force for peace and mutual understanding in our diverse global community.

CHAPTER THREE

WHAT ARE KEY UNIVERSAL THOUGHTS IN ORIENTAL AND WESTERN PHILOSOPHIES ?

Hari Om

Part 1: Introduction

Existential questions have been at the heart of human inquiry since the dawn of consciousness. These questions, which ponder the nature of existence, the purpose of life, the concept of self, and our place in the universe, have been addressed by both Oriental and Western philosophical traditions. Despite their geographical and cultural differences, many common themes emerge when we examine these traditions side by side.

Part 2: The Nature of Reality

Both Oriental and Western philosophies have grappled with understanding the fundamental nature of reality.

Oriental Perspectives:

In many Eastern traditions, reality is often viewed as an interconnected whole. For instance:

1. **Advaita Vedanta (Hinduism):** Proposes the concept of "non-dualism," where ultimate reality (Brahman) is one, and the perception of multiplicity is an illusion (Maya).

2. **Buddhism:** Teaches the concept of "emptiness" (Sunyata), suggesting that all phenomena lack inherent existence and are interdependent.

3. **Taoism:** Presents the idea of Tao as the underlying principle of the universe, emphasizing harmony and balance.

Western Perspectives:

Western philosophy has explored various views on the nature of reality:

1. **Platonic Idealism:** Plato proposed a realm of perfect Forms or Ideas, of which our physical world is but a shadow.

2. **Materialism:** Philosophers like Democritus and later, scientific materialists, argue that reality is fundamentally composed of matter.

3. **Phenomenology:** Husserl and others focused on the study of consciousness and the structures of experience.

Common Theme: Despite differences, both traditions often recognize a distinction between appearance and a deeper reality, and both have streams that emphasize interconnectedness and holism.

Part 3: The Self and Consciousness

The nature of the self and consciousness is another key area of inquiry in both traditions.

Oriental Perspectives:

1. **Buddhism:** Teaches the doctrine of Anatta (no-self), suggesting that there is no permanent, unchanging self.

2. **Hinduism:** While some schools align with the Buddhist view, others like Advaita Vedanta propose an unchanging Atman (self) identical with Brahman.

3. **Confucianism:** Emphasizes the relational nature of the self, defined by one's roles and relationships.

Western Perspectives:

1. **Cartesian Dualism:** Descartes proposed a fundamental distinction between mind and body.

2. **Empiricism:** Locke and Hume questioned the notion of a stable self, with Hume famously unable to find a consistent "I" in his experiences.

3. **Existentialism:** Philosophers like Sartre emphasized individual existence and freedom.

Common Theme: Both traditions have grappled with questions of personal identity, the relationship between mind and body, and the nature of consciousness, often recognizing the complex and potentially illusory nature of the self.

Part 4: Ethics and Morality

Ethical considerations are central to both Oriental and Western philosophical traditions.

Oriental Perspectives:

1. **Buddhism:** Emphasizes compassion and the Eightfold Path as a guide to ethical living.

2. **Confucianism:** Centers on virtues like benevolence (ren) and righteousness (yi).

3. **Hinduism:** Presents the concept of Dharma (duty/ righteousness) as a guide for ethical behavior.

Western Perspectives:

1. **Virtue Ethics:** Aristotle emphasized the cultivation of virtues for a good life.

2. **Deontology:** Kant proposed the categorical imperative as a basis for moral action.

3. **Utilitarianism:** Mill and others argued for maximizing overall happiness or well-being.

Common Theme: Both traditions emphasize the importance of ethical living, often linking it to personal and societal well-being. They also often recognize the complexity of moral decision-making.

Part 5: The Meaning and Purpose of Life

The search for meaning and purpose is a fundamental existential question addressed by both traditions.

Oriental Perspectives:

1. **Buddhism:** Proposes liberation from suffering (Nirvana) as the ultimate goal.

2. Hinduism: Presents various purposes including fulfillment of Dharma, enjoyment (Kama), and ultimately liberation (Moksha).

3. **Taoism:** Emphasizes living in harmony with the Tao.

Western Perspectives:

1. **Existentialism:** Thinkers like Camus and Sartre argued that life has no inherent meaning, and we must create our own.

2. **Eudaimonia:** Aristotle proposed that the purpose of life is to achieve human flourishing.

3. **Religious Perspectives:** Many Western religious philosophies see the purpose of life in relation to God or a divine plan.

Common Theme: Both traditions recognize the human need for meaning and purpose, often linking it to ethical living, personal growth, or transcendent experiences.

Part 6: Knowledge and Truth

The nature of knowledge and truth is another key area of philosophical inquiry in both traditions.

Oriental Perspectives:

1. **Buddhism:** Emphasizes direct experience and meditation as paths to knowledge.

2. **Vedanta:** Recognizes different levels of knowledge, with the highest being direct realization of Brahman.

3. **Taoism:** Often skeptical of conventional knowledge, emphasizing intuitive wisdom.

Western Perspectives:

1. **Rationalism:** Descartes and others emphasized reason as the primary source of knowledge.

2. **Empiricism:** Locke, Hume, and others emphasized sensory experience as the basis of knowledge.

3. **Kant's Synthesis:** Proposed that knowledge arises from both sensory experience and innate structures of the mind.

Common Theme: Both traditions have explored the limits of human knowledge, the relationship between experience and reason, and the possibility of transcendent or intuitive forms of knowing.

Part 7: Time and Temporality

The nature of time and our relationship to it is another area where we see interesting parallels.

Oriental Perspectives:

1. **Hinduism and Buddhism:** Often present cyclical views of time, with concepts like Samsara (cycle of rebirth).

2. **Zen Buddhism:** Emphasizes being present in the moment.

Western Perspectives:

1. **Linear Time:** The Judeo-Christian tradition often presents a linear view of time.

2. **Phenomenology:** Explored the subjective experience of time.

3. **Eternalism vs. Presentism:** Debates in philosophy of time about the nature of past, present, and future.

Common Theme: Both traditions recognize the profound impact of our conception of time on our understanding of existence and often emphasize the importance of one's relationship to the present moment.

Part 8: Freedom and Determinism

The question of free will versus determinism is addressed in various ways in both traditions.

Oriental Perspectives:

1. **Buddhism:** While recognizing causal laws (karma), also emphasizes personal responsibility and the possibility of liberation.

2. **Hinduism:** Various schools have different perspectives, some emphasizing divine will, others individual freedom.

Western Perspectives:

1. **Compatibilism:** Philosophers like Hume argued that free will is compatible with determinism.

2. **Libertarianism:** Argues for a form of free will independent of causal determination.

3. **Hard Determinism:** Argues that all events are caused by prior events, leaving no room for free will.

Common Theme: Both traditions grapple with the tension between causal laws and personal responsibility, often seeking a middle ground or a reframing of the question.

Conclusion:

While Oriental and Western philosophical traditions have developed in different cultural contexts and often use different conceptual frameworks, they have grappled with similar fundamental questions about existence. Both traditions have produced a rich variety of perspectives on these questions, often arriving at surprisingly similar insights despite their different starting points.

The common themes we see emerging include:

1. A recognition of the complexity and potential illusory nature of everyday experience

2. An emphasis on the interconnectedness of all things

3. A focus on ethical living and personal development

4. An exploration of the limits and possibilities of human knowledge

5. A recognition of the profound impact of our conceptions of self, time, and freedom on our lived experience

These commonalities suggest that despite cultural differences, human beings share fundamental existential concerns and have developed sophisticated ways of addressing them across different philosophical traditions. Understanding these common themes can enrich our appreciation of both Oriental and Western philosophy and contribute to meaningful cross-cultural dialogue on life's most profound questions.

CHAPTER FOUR

IMPORTANCE OF SUBJECTIVE EXPERIENCE IN QUEST FOR ULTIMATE REALITY

Hari Om

The distinction between actual realization and objective knowledge is very crucial in the realm of spirituality and the pursuit of ultimate truth.

After getting a bird's eye view of major world religions and philosophies both oriental and western in previous chapters, we articulate a fundamental question.

What could possibly be a pragmatic approach towards balancing objective knowledge with subjective experience ?

In subsequent paragraphs, we attempt consolidation of views from scriptures and contemporary exponents to address how one might balance in life the role of objective knowledge versus subjective experience. We try to understand the role and characterstics of both ie. objective knowledge and subjective experience and how integration of both may help us in seeking ultimate truth.

1. Nature of Ultimate Truth:

Ultimate truth in spirituality often refers to a direct experience or understanding of reality that transcends conceptual knowledge. This truth is frequently described as ineffable, non-dual, or beyond the grasp of the intellectual mind.

2. Limitations of Objective Knowledge:

- **Intellectual Understanding:** Objective knowledge primarily engages the intellect. While valuable, it operates within the realm of duality and conceptual thinking, which many spiritual traditions argue is insufficient for grasping ultimate reality.

- **Second-hand Information:** Objective knowledge often comes from external sources - books, teachers, or scriptures. While these can provide guidance, they remain indirect experiences.

- **Map vs. Territory:** Objective knowledge is akin to having a detailed map of a territory, but never actually visiting the place itself.

3. Nature of Actual Realization:

- **Direct Experience:** Actual realization involves a first-hand, experiential understanding of the truth being sought.

- **Transformation:** It often leads to a fundamental shift in one's perception of reality and sense of self.

- **Beyond Concepts:** Realization transcends intellectual understanding, touching realms of consciousness that words cannot fully capture.

4. The Interplay Between Knowledge and Realization:

- **Preparatory Role:** Objective knowledge can serve as a crucial foundation, providing context and direction for the seeker.

- **Guidance:** It can help avoid common pitfalls and misunderstandings in the spiritual journey.

- **Verification:** After realization, objective knowledge can help integrate and articulate the experience.

5. Why Actual Realization is Crucial:

- **Embodiment:** Realization allows the seeker to embody the truth, not just understand it conceptually.

- **Lasting Transformation:** While knowledge can be forgotten, genuine realization fundamentally alters one's being.
- **Breaking Through Limitations:** Realization can shatter deeply ingrained beliefs and perceptions that objective knowledge alone might not touch.

6. Challenges in Pursuing Realization:

- **Mistaking Knowledge for Realization:** There's a risk of believing that accumulated knowledge equals spiritual attainment.
- **Ego Traps:** The pursuit of realization can ironically strengthen the ego if not approached with humility.
- **Impatience:** The desire for quick results can lead to superficial experiences mistaken for deep realization.

7. Methods for Cultivating Realization:

- Meditation and Contemplation: Practices that quiet the mind and allow for direct perception.
- Self-Inquiry: Techniques that investigate the nature of the self and reality.
- Devotion: Some traditions emphasize surrender and devotion as paths to realization.
- Mindfulness: Bringing awareness to everyday experiences can lead to profound insights.

8. Integration of Knowledge and Realization:

- Balancing Act: The most effective spiritual paths often combine intellectual understanding with practices aimed at direct realization.
- Iterative Process: Knowledge can lead to experiences, which then deepen understanding, creating a positive feedback loop.

9. Cultural and Traditional Perspectives:

- **Eastern Traditions:** Many Eastern spiritual paths, like Buddhism and Advaita Vedanta, strongly emphasize the importance of direct realization over mere knowledge.
- **Western Mysticism:** Similarly, Western mystical traditions often speak of the limitations of intellectual knowledge in grasping divine truths.

Views of Contemporary Spiritual Teachers:

1. Swami Vivekananda:

In his work "Raja Yoga," Swami Vivekananda emphasizes:

"The goal of all science is to find unity... Religion will be the science which will find the fundamental unity in all religions... But we have to go beyond the material plane... to know the Self, to go beyond all the senses; this is the goal of all science and religion."

This underscores the importance of direct experience beyond intellectual understanding.

2. Sri Aurobindo:

In "The Life Divine," Sri Aurobindo writes:

"The supreme Truth is not a principle that can be captured by thought... It has to be lived, realized in our entire being."

3. Paramahansa Yogananda:

In "Autobiography of a Yogi," he states:

"The rishis discovered that man's earthly and heavenly environment, in all its manifestations, is governed by laws intelligible to reason; and that the harmony of the universe is guided by mathematical measurements. The discovery of these laws gave birth to various sciences. The Hindu scriptures place the greatest emphasis on man's own experience as the final proof of the truth."

4. Sri Ramana Maharshi, a revered 20th-century Indian sage, often spoke about the relationship between knowledge and realization. In "Talks with Sri Ramana Maharshi," he states:

"Book-learning is useful up to a certain point. But it cannot take us to our goal. After a certain stage, we must put book-learning aside and enter into practice."

This perspective acknowledges the value of knowledge while emphasizing the primacy of direct experience.

5. Eckhart Tolle, in his book "The Power of Now," emphasizes:

"To know yourself as the Being underneath the thinker, the stillness underneath the mental noise, the love and joy underneath the pain, is freedom, salvation, enlightenment."

This quote underscores the difference between intellectual understanding and direct realization of one's true nature.

6. Adyashanti, a modern spiritual teacher, states in "The End of Your World":

"Enlightenment is a destructive process. It has nothing to do with becoming better or being happier. Enlightenment is the crumbling away of untruth. It's seeing through the facade of pretense. It's the complete eradication of everything we imagined to be true."

This perspective highlights how realization often involves a radical shift beyond mere accumulation of knowledge.

Hindu Scriptures on Direct Experience:

1. Bhagavad Gita:

"But those who, worshipping Me with love, meditate on My formless aspect, having restrained all their senses, and being even-minded everywhere, they indeed reach Me." (Chapter 12, Verse 3-4)

This verse emphasizes direct experience through meditation and devotion.

2. Yoga Sutras of Patanjali:

"Atha yoga anushasanam" - "Now, the teachings of yoga." (Sutra 1.1) This opening sutra implies that yoga is a practical discipline, not just theoretical knowledge.

3. Mundaka Upanishad:

"This Atman cannot be attained by study of the Vedas, or by intelligence, or by much hearing of sacred books. It is attained by him alone whom It chooses. To such a one Atman reveals Its own form." (3.2.3)

4. Brahma Sutras:

"Brahman is known only from the scriptures and not independently by any other means is established, because it is the main purport (of all Vedantic texts)." (1.1.3)

While this might seem to contradict direct experience, traditional commentators interpret this to mean that **scriptures point the way, but direct realization is still necessary.**

5. Vivekachudamani (attributed to Adi Shankara):

"Neither by Yoga, nor by Sankhya, nor by work, nor by learning, but by the realization of one's identity with Brahman is Liberation possible, and by no other means." (Verse 56)

6. Katha Upanishad states:

"This Self cannot be attained by instruction, nor by intellectual power, nor even through much hearing. It is attained by him alone whom It chooses. To such a one, the Self reveals Its own nature." (Katha Upanishad 1.2.23)

7. In Buddhism, the Lankavatara Sutra emphasizes:

"Words are not the highest reality, nor is what is expressed in words the highest reality. Why? Because the highest reality is an exalted state of bliss, and as it is beyond thinking, it is not a state of word-discrimination."

These scriptural references underscore the limitations of verbal or conceptual knowledge in grasping ultimate truth.

Scientific Perspectives:

While not strictly spiritual, neuroscientific research on meditation and altered states of consciousness provides interesting parallels. For instance, studies on long-term meditators show structural changes in the brain, suggesting that consistent practice leads to tangible transformations beyond mere intellectual understanding.

Role of knowledge and direct experience in our search for final answers:

The relationship between knowledge and direct experience of ultimate reality is a nuanced one, and different traditions have varying perspectives:

1. Complementary Roles:

Many traditions see knowledge and experience as complementary. Knowledge can provide a map or framework, while direct experience provides the actual terrain. For instance:

- In Buddhism, theoretical understanding (pariyatti) is seen as a foundation for practice (patipatti), which leads to realization (pativedha).

- In Hindu Vedanta, knowledge (jnana) is often seen as a path to direct realization (anubhava) of ultimate reality.

2. Limitations of Conceptual Knowledge:

Many traditions, particularly in the East, warn about the limitations of purely conceptual knowledge:

- Zen Buddhism emphasizes direct experience over intellectual understanding.
- Taoism often critiques conventional knowledge, favoring intuitive wisdom.
- Western mystics like Meister Eckhart have similarly emphasized the inadequacy of concepts to capture ultimate reality.

3. The Role of Practice:

Most traditions that emphasize direct experience of ultimate reality also emphasize the importance of spiritual practices or disciplines:

- Meditation and contemplative practices in various traditions.
- Yoga in Hinduism.
- Contemplative prayer in Christian mysticism.

4. Integration of Knowledge and Experience:

Some modern approaches emphasize integrating intellectual understanding with experiential practices:

- Transpersonal psychology attempts to bridge spiritual experiences with psychological understanding.
- Some contemporary spiritual teachers (e.g., Ken Wilber) advocate for an integral approach that combines intellectual knowledge, experiential practices, and ethical living.

In conclusion, while knowledge provides an important foundation and framework, many traditions suggest that direct experience of ultimate reality is indeed "the way forward" for deepest understanding and transformation. However, this doesn't negate the value of knowledge; rather, it suggests a complementary approach.

For modern life, this might mean:

1. Cultivating a solid intellectual understanding of philosophical and spiritual concepts.
2. Engaging in regular contemplative or mindfulness practices.
3. Seeking experiences that transcend ordinary consciousness (through meditation, nature immersion, art, etc.)

4. Integrating insights from these experiences into daily ethical living.

5. Maintaining an attitude of openness, humility, and continuous learning, recognizing that both our knowledge and our experiences are always partial and evolving.

This approach allows for a rich, multifaceted engagement with life that honors both the intellectual and experiential dimensions of human existence, potentially leading to a more fulfilled and meaningful life in our complex modern world.

In conclusion, while objective knowledge plays a vital role in the spiritual journey, actual realization is often considered the ultimate goal for seekers of truth. It represents a shift from knowing about reality to directly experiencing and embodying it. The journey typically involves a dance between acquiring knowledge and cultivating direct experience, with the understanding that true wisdom arises from the integration of both.

CHAPTER FIVE

SEARCH FOR AN EASY PATH TO TRUE KNOWLEDGE

Hari Om

Having understood in previous chapters, the key themes running through major world religions and philosophies both oriental and western, we attempt to articulate key attributes of an easy path that attempts intergration of objective knowledge and direct subjective experience towards realisation of our true nature.

Part 1: Introduction

The quest for true knowledge, or "jnana" in Sanskrit, has been a central theme in Hindu philosophy for thousands of years. The Hindu tradition offers various paths towards this ultimate understanding, some more accessible than others. In this chapter, we'll explore an approach that is considered relatively easy or straightforward, while still being deeply rooted in ancient wisdom.

It's important to note that in Hindu philosophy, true knowledge is not merely intellectual understanding, but a direct, experiential realization of the ultimate reality. This reality is often referred to as Brahman, the universal consciousness that underlies all existence.

Part 2: The Concept of "Easy Path" in Hindu Thought

The idea of an "easy path" to spiritual realization is not foreign to Hindu philosophy. In fact, several traditions within Hinduism have emphasized more accessible approaches to spiritual growth, particularly in response to the needs of householders and those unable to pursue more demanding ascetic practices.

1. Bhakti Yoga: Often considered one of the most accessible paths, Bhakti Yoga focuses on devotion and love for the Divine.

2. Karma Yoga: This path emphasizes selfless action and duty as a means to spiritual growth.

3. Jnana Yoga: While traditionally considered a demanding path, some schools have developed more accessible approaches to self-inquiry and knowledge.

4. Mantra Yoga: The use of sacred sounds or phrases as a focus for meditation and spiritual growth.

The approach we'll explore draws elements from these traditions, with a particular emphasis on accessible practices that can be integrated into daily life.

Part 3: Foundations of the Easy Path

The easy path towards true knowledge in Hindu wisdom is built on several key principles:

1. **Simplicity:** The practices and concepts should be straightforward and easy to understand.

2. **Integration with Daily Life:** The path should be compatible with the responsibilities of a householder.

3. **Gradual Progress:** It recognizes that spiritual growth is often a gradual process rather than a sudden transformation.

4. **Emphasis on Direct Experience:** While study is important, the focus is on practices that lead to direct spiritual experiences.

5. **Holistic Approach:** It addresses the physical, mental, emotional, and spiritual aspects of the individual.

Part 4: The Role of a Guru

In Hindu tradition, the role of a spiritual teacher or guru is often considered crucial. However, the easy path recognizes that not everyone has access to a personal guru. Therefore, it emphasizes:

1. **Self-study (Svadhyaya):** Regular study of spiritual texts and teachings.

2. **Inner Guidance:** Developing the ability to listen to one's inner wisdom.

3. **Community Support:** Engaging with like-minded individuals for support and shared learning.

4. **Respect for Tradition:** While a personal guru might not be available, respecting and learning from the lineage of teachers is important.

Part 5: Key Practices of the Easy Path

1. Meditation (Dhyana):

a) Start with short, regular sessions (e.g., 10-15 minutes daily)

b) Focus on simple techniques like breath awareness or mantra repetition

c) Gradually increase duration and depth of practice

2. Self-Inquiry (Atma Vichara):

a) Regular contemplation on questions like "Who am I?"

b) Observing thoughts and emotions without attachment

c) Cultivating witness consciousness

3. Devotional Practices (Bhakti):

a) Choosing a personal deity or form of the Divine

b) Daily prayer or puja (worship ritual)

c) Cultivating an attitude of surrender and love

4. Mindful Action (Karma Yoga):

a) Performing daily duties with full attention and without attachment to results

b) Cultivating an attitude of service

c) Practicing non-violence (ahimsa) in thoughts, words, and actions

5. Study of Scriptures (Svadhyaya):

a) Regular reading of texts like the Bhagavad Gita, Upanishads, or other spiritual literature

b) Reflection on the teachings and their application in daily life

c) Discussing insights with others on the path

6. Mantra Practice:

a) Choosing a mantra (e.g., Om, So'ham, or a deity's name)

b) Regular japa (mantra repetition) using mala beads

c) Integrating mantra with daily activities

7. Cultivating Virtues:

a) Focus on developing qualities like compassion, truthfulness, and contentment

b) Regular self-reflection on one's progress

c) Practicing forgiveness and letting go of negativity

Part 6: The Role of the Body

Hindu wisdom recognizes the importance of the physical body in spiritual practice. The easy path includes:

1. **Yoga Asanas:** Simple physical postures to keep the body healthy and energy flowing

2. **Pranayama:** Basic breathing exercises to balance the life force

3. **Proper Diet:** Following a sattvic (pure) diet that supports spiritual practice

4. **Adequate Rest:** Ensuring proper sleep and relaxation to support the practice

Part 7: Stages of Progress

The easy path recognizes several stages of spiritual progress:

1. **Awakening:** Initial interest in spiritual matters and recognition of a higher reality

2. **Purification:** Clearing mental and emotional obstacles through practice

3. **Illumination:** Glimpses of higher states of consciousness and spiritual insights

4. **Stabilization:** Consistent experience of expanded awareness in daily life

5. **Liberation:** Complete realization of one's true nature as universal consciousness

It's important to note that progress is often non-linear, with individuals moving back and forth between stages.

Part 8: Overcoming Obstacles

The easy path acknowledges common obstacles and provides strategies to overcome them:

1. **Lack of Time:** Emphasizing short, regular practices integrated into daily life

2. **Mental Restlessness:** Gradual training of the mind through meditation and mindfulness

3. **Doubt:** Encouraging study, contemplation, and seeking clarification from teachers or texts

4. **Lack of Motivation:** Cultivating satsang (spiritual company) and regular inspiration through study

5. **Attachment to Results:** Emphasizing the importance of practice for its own sake, rather than for specific outcomes

Part 9: The Role of Grace

While the easy path emphasizes personal effort, it also recognizes the role of divine grace or "anugraha." This is seen as a supportive force that aids the seeker's progress. Practices to cultivate receptivity to grace include:

1. **Surrender (Ishvara Pranidhana):** Letting go of ego and trusting in a higher power

2. **Gratitude:** Cultivating thankfulness for all experiences, both pleasant and challenging

3. **Openness:** Maintaining an attitude of receptivity to spiritual guidance and insights

Part 10: Integration with Daily Life

A key aspect of the easy path is its integration with everyday activities:

1. **Mindful Work:** Treating one's profession or daily tasks as a form of spiritual practice

2. **Conscious Relationships:** Viewing interactions with others as opportunities for spiritual growth

3. **Nature Connection:** Cultivating awareness of the divine in the natural world

4. **Artistic Expression:** Using creative activities as a form of spiritual practice

5. **Conscious Consumption:** Being mindful of what one consumes (food, media, experiences) and its impact on spiritual growth

Part 11: The Importance of Balance

The easy path emphasizes the importance of balance in spiritual practice:

1. **Effort and Relaxation:** Balancing disciplined practice with periods of rest and integration

2. **Solitude and Community:** Combining personal practice with supportive relationships

3. **Study and Experience:** Balancing intellectual understanding with direct spiritual experience

4. **Inner Work and Outer Action:** Combining contemplative practices with engaged action in the world

Part 12: Markers of Progress

While the ultimate goal is beyond conceptual understanding, the easy path recognizes certain markers of spiritual progress:

1. **Increased Peace:** A growing sense of inner calm and equanimity

2. **Expanded Awareness:** A broader perspective on life and one's place in the universe

3. **Deepening Compassion:** Growing concern for the well-being of all beings

4. **Reduced Reactivity:** Less automatic reaction to life's ups and downs

5. **Intuitive Wisdom:** Increased access to inner guidance and insight

6. **Joy and Contentment:** A growing sense of fulfillment independent of external circumstances

Part 13: The Role of Symbolism and Ritual

While emphasizing simplicity, the easy path recognizes the power of symbolism and ritual in spiritual practice:

1. **Personal Altar:** Creating a sacred space for daily practice

2. **Use of Symbols:** Incorporating meaningful spiritual symbols into one's environment

3. **Simple Rituals:** Developing personal rituals that support spiritual focus

4. Sacred Times: Recognizing auspicious times (e.g., dawn, dusk) for intensified practice

Part 14: Adapting Ancient Wisdom to Modern Life

The easy path seeks to make ancient Hindu wisdom accessible to modern practitioners:

1. **Technology Integration:** Using apps or online resources to support practice

2. **Scientific Understanding:** Incorporating insights from fields like neuroscience to understand the effects of spiritual practices

3. **Psychological Integration:** Recognizing the interplay between psychological healing and spiritual growth

4. **Global Perspective:** Embracing a universal spirituality while respecting Hindu roots

Part 15: The Ultimate Goal

While the path is described as "easy," it's important to remember that the ultimate goal in Hindu philosophy is profound:

1. **Self-Realization:** Direct experience of one's true nature as universal consciousness

2. **Liberation (Moksha):** Freedom from the cycle of birth and death

3. **Unity Consciousness:** Recognition of the fundamental oneness of all existence

4. **Divine Love:** Experiencing unconditional love for all beings

Part 16: Conclusion

The easy path towards true knowledge in Hindu wisdom offers a accessible approach to spiritual growth rooted in ancient tradition. By emphasizing simplicity, integration with daily life, and direct experience, it provides a framework for individuals to progress towards self-realization while fulfilling their worldly responsibilities.

This path recognizes that while the ultimate goal is profound, the journey itself can be approached with ease, joy, and gradual, steady progress. It honors the essence of Hindu wisdom while adapting to the needs and circumstances of modern practitioners.

Ultimately, the easy path is not about avoiding challenges, but about approaching spiritual growth with an attitude of openness, patience, and trust in the process. It recognizes that true knowledge is not just intellectual understanding, but a lived experience of our deepest nature and our connection to all of existence.

By following this path with sincerity and persistence, practitioners can gradually unfold their inner potential, leading to a life of greater wisdom, compassion, and fulfillment. The journey towards true knowledge becomes not just a distant goal, but a daily experience of growth and discovery.

The generic approach suggested in this chapter has to be supplemented by a more detailed account on possible methodology by a seeker. The next few chapters provide this methodology using authentic Vedantic texts and Patanjali Yoga Sutras. Patanjali Yoga Sutras focus more on practice than the concepts available in Vedanta philosophy. These final chapters have been adapted from an earlier book by the author titled ' Explore within Self for Meaning of Life'.

CHAPTER SIX

HOW DO I PROGRESS ON THE PATH TO REALISE ULTIMATE TRUTH?

Hari Om

Chapter 5 has provided the approach followed in Hinduism to progress spiritually. But there are many practical difficulties to be resolved before one can see some tangible results.

It is important to understand that this inward journey is a leap of faith. Faith denotes our mental state to trust something. In the physical world we use an elevator in a multi-story building, as we have faith about its safe operation. We undertake air travel because of faith in the aviation industry safety norms. Most of our relationships with others are based on faith.

In the physical world we are able to evaluate the evidence about the underpinning of our faiths on various things using our senses , mind and intellect.

In Spiritual pursuits our senses , mind -intellect system does not seem to help. Our spiritual self is hypothesized to be beyond them and is supposed to be a passive observer of the activities of the physical world including our body-mind complex. So what is the big deal in connecting with this passive true self?

The answer provided by scriptures is that if we change our identification from our body and mind to this spiritual self, many strange things happen.

We find that all our sorrows and fears that are rooted in and caused by our body and mind seem to disappear. It is like waking up from a bad dream. The experience is very liberating and persists for all time to come. It is also called Moksha.

The reason for our identification with body-mind is ignorance or Avidya, as described in our scriptures. This ignorance can only be removed by knowledge or Jnana.

Thus Jnana (Knowledge)Yoga is the only way through which liberation from ignorance is possible. However, there is a catch; one can practice Jnana yoga using a tool of meditation only if our mind is purified from various past impressions that cause continuous turbulence and are roadblocks to our meeting with Spiritual self.

So this seems to be a catch 22 situation. How do we get out of it?

In Gita, Krishna provides a blue print for action.

He talks of Karma Yoga at length to Arjun. Some ignorant people mistakenly accuse Him to have put Arjun on the path of War rather than Peace. Arjun wanted to pursue peace at onset of the battle because of his misplaced attachment to relatives in the opposing army. It is very important to understand the nuances of Karma Yoga.

Karma Yoga is supposed to act as a cleaning agent to our mind and a clean mind is a precondition for embarking on Jnana Yoga through meditation practices.

Many approaches for success in Karma Yoga are provided by way of Dos and Don't , in the form of Yama and Niyam.

Plot is simple. If you want a postgraduate degree you have to start from primary school. If you want to climb a mountain, base camps are a necessary evil. Spirituality does not come easily. We need to have a commitment to our cherished goal and desire to face the challenges in the path.

So this journey needs preparation in terms of understanding background concepts and some behavioral changes to prepare our body and mind.

We plan to use the guidance of the Indian Vedanta system for this preparation. The Upanishads, the Bhagavad-Gita and the Brahma Sutra constitute the basis of Vedanta. All schools of Vedanta propound their philosophy by interpreting these texts, collectively called the Prasthana Trayi, literally, three sources.

Bhagavad-Gita , which is part of epic Mahabharat is a discourse given by Lord Krishna to Arjun in the battle field and is considered a very renowned source of learning the concepts of Spirituality.

Like in the battlefield of Kurukshetra, in our daily life too we face challenging situations as faced by Arjun. We get confused about our proper reaction to the conflicting stimuli impacting us. In dealing with such dilemma one is advised to follow one's specified Dharma (Duty).

The Bhagavad Gita offers profound insights and guidance on the paths of Karma Yoga (the yoga of action) and Jnana Yoga (the yoga of knowledge). Here are some key learnings from the Gita on these two yogas:

Karma Yoga:

1. Perform actions as a sacred duty without attachment to the fruits of actions (2.47).

2. Work without desire for personal rewards, possessiveness, or egotistical motives (2.49).

3. Equanimity - remain balanced in success and failure, pleasure and pain (2.38).

4. Dedicate all actions to the Divine as an offering without ownership (3.30).

5. Renounce the fruits of actions to attain peace and freedom from bondage (5.12).

6. Work with discipline, without likes and dislikes, for self-purification (18.6).

Jnana Yoga:

1. Discriminate between the temporary material body and the eternal Atman (soul) (2.16).

2. Gain spiritual wisdom by overcoming ignorance and attachments (4.39).

3. Realize the indestructible, immutable, and eternal nature of the Atman (2.20).

4. Understand that the Atman is the true self, distinct from the mind and senses (3.42).

5. Practice meditation, self-study, and contemplation to steady the mind (6.35).

6. Develop equal vision towards all beings, seeing the one Divine in everything (6.29).

7. Conquer the mind and senses through knowledge and detachment (3.43).

8. Attain the supreme knowledge of the imperishable Brahman (the Absolute) (18.50).

Additionally, the Gita emphasizes the harmony of Karma Yoga and Jnana Yoga, where selfless action purifies the mind, leading to spiritual knowledge and eventual liberation. The essence is to act without attachment and perform one's duties with an attitude of offering it to the Divine, while simultaneously cultivating self-knowledge and realizing one's true identity as the eternal Atman.

Meditation

The various approaches to meditation can help us achieve peace of mind and the ability to act with equanimity in the world in the following ways:

1. Concentration/Focused Meditation:

This involves techniques like breath awareness, mantra repetition, or gazing at an object. By training the mind to remain focused, we learn to control the wandering tendencies and develop one-pointedness. This helps cultivate mental clarity, stability, and calmness in the face of external circumstances.

2. Mindfulness/Open Monitoring Meditation:

Practices like Vipassana or Zen meditation cultivate non-judgmental, present-moment awareness of our thoughts, emotions, and sensations as they arise. This allows us to disengage from ruminative patterns, develop detachment, and respond to situations with more objectivity and equanimity.

3. Loving-Kindness/Compassion Meditation:

By cultivating feelings of unconditional love, compassion, and goodwill towards ourselves and others, we overcome negative emotions like anger, hatred, and aversion. This fosters a sense of interconnectedness, empathy, and the ability to act with kindness and equanimity.

4. Analytical Meditation:

Contemplating profound philosophical teachings or analyzing the nature of the self, impermanence, and interdependence can lead to insights that free us from afflictive mental states and attachments. This wisdom nurtures equanimity and peace.

5. Devotional Meditation:

By cultivating feelings of love, devotion, and surrender to the Divine/Absolute, we transcend our limited sense of self and develop trust, faith, and inner peace, enabling us to face life's challenges with acceptance and equanimity.

6. Movement/Embodied Meditation:

Practices like Yoga, Tai Chi, or walking meditation help develop body awareness, grounding, and integration of mind-body. This holistic approach harmonizes our inner state, promoting a sense of centered presence and equanimity.

Across traditions, meditation aims to train the mind, transform our perspective, and help us respond to life's vicissitudes with a balanced, peaceful, and compassionate mindset, ultimately enabling us to act with wisdom and equanimity in the world.

However, the above information is of no use to us unless we follow a structured approach to self realization.

Panch Kosh Vivek is a technique to be described in next chapter that helps us get a perspective.

Patanjali Yoga Sutra provides Ashtanga Yoga (eight limbed Yoga) to help seeker move forward in a systematic manner. We shall describe it too after Panch kosh (Five Layers) Vivek, which attempts to break our personality into five layers to get an idea of our true self.

Online Resources:

Karma Yoga, Jnana Yoga, Meditation, Vedanta
https://youtu.be/AawWsJNi0gM?si=_l1rZNbw58hG4DiK
https://youtu.be/wm9gomNUi48?si=vpBiCCcOddERE_an
https://youtu.be/-rgNWIeF9Qo?si=bZuL3MHorWjfljhd
https://youtu.be/EijmfagFw20?si=3RbXyaNXKg0AkrB6

CHAPTER SEVEN

GETTING TO THE BASICS OF HINDUISM

Hari Om

"The Self is beyond all sense-objects, beyond the universal and its effects, beyond this universe of duality and non-duality. It is that which remains after all else is cast away." - Kaushitaki Upanishad

Before we can explore concepts of Panch Kosh (Five Sheaths) of our personality, and embark on the journey prescribed by Patanjali in his famous Yoga Sutra, we need to be familiar with the concept of rebirth. Hindu scriptures are very clear about the concept of Moksha which is nothing but cessation of the continuous cycle of rebirth.

Is Moksha really worth pursuing?

Many of us are perfectly happy with what life offers; after all it has happy events and sorrows come and go. They may not like the idea of Moksha. It is only those who have developed aversion to the mixed bag that life offers, who are likely to seek Spiritual self.

For such seekers, there is assurance that whatever effort is put towards that goal of Moksha does not go waste and the seeker may achieve it over several lifetimes. Every rebirth begins from a higher state and closer to the ultimate goal.

Concept of Rebirth:

The philosophy of rebirth or reincarnation (punarjanma) is based on the belief that the soul (atman/jiva) is eternal and undergoes a cycle of birth, death, and rebirth. After death, the subtle body containing the mind, intellect, and impressions (samskaras) carries the cumulative effect of one's karma and becomes the cause for the next incarnation. The nature and circumstances of the new birth are determined by the cumulative karmas of the previous lives, manifesting as tendencies, abilities, and life situations. Karma is thus the driving force behind the cycle of rebirth (samsara) until one attains moksha (liberation) by exhausting all karmas.

Role of Samskaras:

Samskaras refer to the subtle impressions, habitual tendencies, and karmic imprints carried over from previous lives in the form of latent desires and inclinations. These samskaras shape an individual's personality, natural talents, proclivities, and the karmic baggage that determines the nature of rebirth.

Samskaras are formed by the countless thoughts, emotions, and actions performed over numerous lifetimes. They act as the subtle driving forces that influence one's behaviors, circumstances, and the path of future incarnations until they are fully resolved or expended.

The goal of spiritual practice in Hinduism is to burn or exhaust all accumulated samskaras and karmas through right living, self-discipline, selfless service, and ultimately, the attainment of self-knowledge (atma-jnana) to break free from the cycle of rebirth and attain moksha or liberation.

According to Hindu philosophy, our past life samskaras (impressions/tendencies) play a significant role in shaping our current life events and circumstances, while also allowing for the exercise of free will on the spiritual path towards self-realization.

Persistence of Past Life Samskaras:

The cumulative impressions and karmic traces (samskaras) from our past lives are carried over into the present birth through the subtle body (linga sharira/sukshma sharira).

These samskaras manifest as innate tendencies, personality traits, inclinations, talents, and even challenges or handicaps we face in this life.

They influence our thought patterns, emotional responses, desires, and the karmic situations we encounter, acting as the unseen forces that shape many aspects of our life events. However, samskaras are not viewed as an inescapable destiny, but rather as the starting point or field of play in the present life.

Free Will and Conscious Effort:

While past samskaras exert their influence, Hindu scriptures emphasize that human beings possess free will (Sanskrit: purushakara) and the ability to make conscious choices. Through conscious effort, discrimination (viveka), self-discipline (sadacara), and spiritual practice (sadhana), one can gradually overcome negative samskaras and cultivate positive impressions.

The practice of karma yoga (selfless action), jnana yoga (path of knowledge), and bhakti yoga (path of devotion) are means to purify the mind and attenuate the hold of past samskaras.

Ultimately, it is through the realization of one's true nature as the eternal Self (Atman/Brahman) that one becomes free from the bondage of samskaras altogether.

Shaping Destiny on the Spiritual Path:

On the spiritual path, a sincere seeker is encouraged to exercise free will by making conscious choices that align with dharma (righteous conduct) and lead towards self-realization.

Each thought, action, and effort undertaken with awareness and right intention creates new positive samskaras that counteract and gradually erase the negative past impressions.

The guidance of a guru (spiritual teacher) and the study of scriptures help the seeker develop viveka (discriminative wisdom) to navigate the spiritual journey more effectively.

Persistent effort, self-effort (purushartha), and the grace of the Divine are considered vital in reshaping one's destiny towards the ultimate goal of moksha (liberation).

Thus, while past life samskaras exert their influence, Hindu thought emphasizes the pivotal role of freewill, conscious effort, and spiritual practice in gradually overcoming these karmic impressions and shaping one's destiny towards self-realization and transcendence of all bondage. **Figure 1** attempts to capture this concept. The process is played out iteratively over several life times till one reaches self-realization and subsequent moksha.

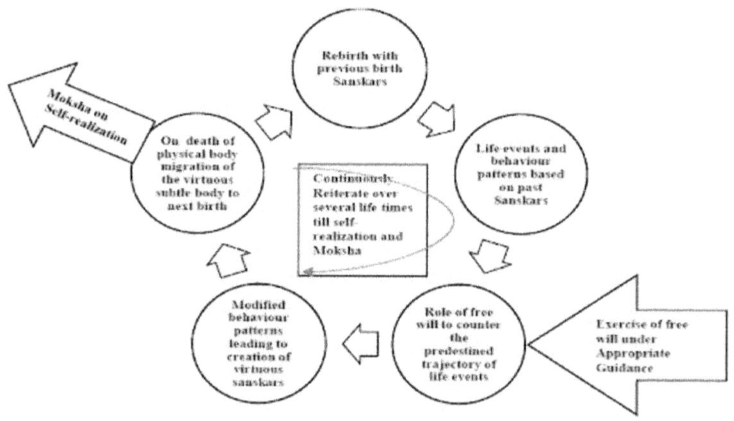

Fig 1 :Role of free will to cancel the negative samskaras and Moksha on self-realization

Having understood the concept of rebirth and the possibility of escaping this perpetual cycle of birth and death by taking steps under appropriate guidance towards self-realization and eventual Moksha or Nirvana, now it would be logical to know what our true self is and where to find it.

The Taittiriya Upanishad, a revered ancient Hindu scripture, provides us a perspective on our true nature using a process called Panch Kosh (Five Sheath) vivek ; a discrimination method.

The Concept of Ananda:

The Taittiriya Upanishad introduces the concept of Ananda, which goes beyond mere happiness or pleasure. It describes

Ananda as the inherent bliss that permeates all existence, beyond the realm of fleeting emotions. The Upanishad encourages us to seek this eternal bliss by realizing our true nature, transcending the limitations of the material world.

The Five Sheaths (Pancha Koshas):

The Taittiriya Upanishad presents the idea of Pancha Koshas, the five sheaths that envelop the true self. These sheaths include the physical body, vital energy, the mind, intellect, and the blissful core of being. By understanding and transcending these layers, one can delve deeper into their true essence and establish a profound connection with the divine. The true self is beyond all the five sheaths including Anandmaya kosha or blissful core . Anandmaya kosha is our staging stage for self realization of true self. One does not stay at this blissful core and by developing detachment to this blissful layer too, we transcend to the ultimate goal of self realization.

This process is akin to peeling layers of an onion. So what do we find at the core of the onion? Really nothing that we can see. Similarly when we start peeling these layers of our personality using the Panch Kosh vivek process, we don't find any object as our true self. So is the search futile ? Not really. Our true self is the one who is actually doing the peeling. It is aware of all the five layers. It is the observer of these five layers. It is the consciousness itself. All the five layers are manifestations of that true self and function only because of the core of consciousness within. All layers of the onion are a manifestation of onion only. Similarly all aspects (sheaths) of our personality are manifestations of the spiritual self. The waves of the ocean are the ocean itself ; all are full of water. All ornaments are nothing but gold.

Figure 2 attempts to describe our journey from body consciousness to realization of our true nature (Atma) by transcending the five koshas or layers of body-mind apparatus.

Figure 3 is attempting to show pictorially the inter-relationship of five sheaths; with gross level Annamaya Kosha (our physical body) being the outermost ring and subtler constituents are reached as we move inward. The true self (Atman) is at the very core.

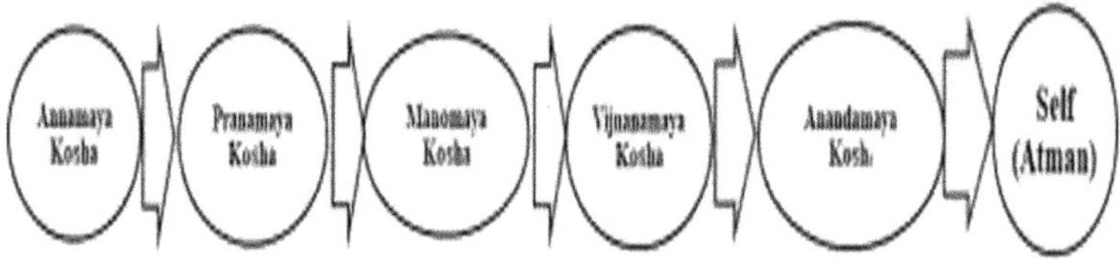

Fig 2 : Process of Panch Kosha Vivek to realization of Self from body consciousness

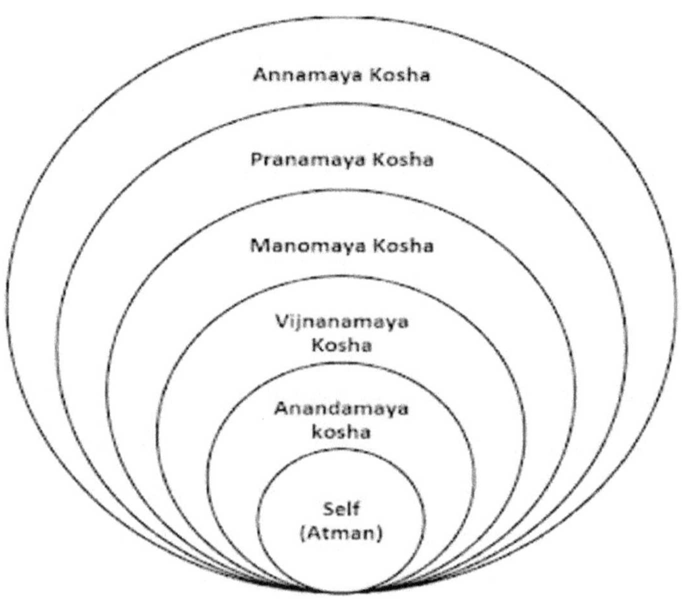

Fig 3 : The pictorial view of five Sheaths that constitute our personality

The teaching of Pancha Kosha Viveka states that the true Self (Atman) is distinct from these five sheaths or coverings. These sheaths veil or obscure the realization of the Atman. The goal of self-realization is to transcend each of these sheaths or layers of existence, and ultimately realize one's true identity through the blissful Anandamaya Kosha - the Atman, which is one with Brahman (the Absolute Reality).

The process of Panch Kosh Vivek involves:

a. Recognizing each sheath for what it is through discrimination (viveka). We need to read scriptures, listen to people who have the ability to guide us and introspect in silence. The process is slow and tedious but certainly worth the effort.

b.Withdrawing identification from each outer sheath as "not the Self." One key attribute of our True Self is that it is changeless. All sheaths that are manifested out of it are changing with time. Our body ages, our mind changes at a pace that is phenomenal, our intellect too changes. A Goldsmith during evaluation of gold ornaments' value is looking at the gold substrate only ; he can create different designs of ornaments but gold is changeless. The value is of Gold. Likewise value is of changeless Self.

c. Steadily moving inward until one realizes the bliss sheath of pure consciousness as one's true nature. As we move forward we experience subtler aspects of our personality. The happiness that we experience in our day to day existence ; be it from a good meal or other body pleasures, all are nothing but trickles from this bliss sheath. If we can remain in bliss sheath continuously, we go through life in a state of flow.

By peeling off these sheaths, one moves from ignorance (avidya) to Self-knowledge (Atma Jnana). The source of our ignorance is to seek permanence in a changing world. The difference between unchanging (Sat) and changing (Asat) has to be understood by deep contemplation. Journey of Self realization is to develop the ability to discriminate 'Sat' from 'Asat'. The Upanishads guide the seeker to look within and directly experience in the Anandamaya Kosha - the blissful Self that is eternal, changeless, and one with the ultimate Brahman. It is to be clearly understood that Anandmaya kosha is only a staging ground for self realization and one has to go beyond it to reach ultimate goal of liberation.

In The Journal of Transpersonal Psychology, 2016, Vol. 48, No. 2, Maharaj K. Raina in his article "THE LEVELS OF HUMAN CONSCIOUSNESS AND CREATIVE FUNCTIONING: INSIGHTS FROM THE THEORY OF PANCHA KOSHA (FIVE SHEATHS OF CONSCIOUSNESS)", describes these sheaths very elaborately and the following text is an adaption from this article.

Annamaya kosha

The outermost layer, the Annamaya kosha, the food sheath or 'food body,' is a representation of the gross physical body, considered as primitive and the least powerful part of the persona. This sheath is regarded as the medium of enjoyment for gross objects through the physical senses. All living beings in this world are born from food and remain alive by the consumption of food. It is the external body, made of matter, like other objects seen outside by our gross senses. Here, matter is called 'food', thus conceiving it organically. This sheath is concerned with our physical existence: birth, growth, change, death and decay are its qualities.

Pranamaya Kosha

The second covering of the Self is the pranamaya kosha or vital sheath consisting of the five pranas or vital energies and the five karma indriyas or organs of action. This level of being is associated with the breath, the prana, and the fundamental lifeforce. It is also associated with feelings and emotions. This is a template of concentrated life force (prana). Prana, in its universal aspect, underlies all physical and mental processes. It stands specifically for the field of energy that penetrates and surrounds the physical body and has variously been styled 'astral body,' 'etheric double,' and 'plasma body.' It is the medium of exchange in the whole psychophysiological system. Prana is the life force of the persona responsible for the various physiological functions within the body, and it plays a critical role as the mediating link between body and mind. In the conscious state one experiences prana, when it is manifested in the form of the breath . Here, energy is also described as prana, which means 'living breath.' The Upanishads prescribe various meditations on prana to raise consciousness from the body to a higher level of the life force. Those who can identify with this powerhouse of energy attain great control over the body; they spontaneously experience a new feeling of freedom, strength, and joy. Consciousness on the level of the Pranamaya kosha is more subtle and powerful than that of the first covering, the Annamaya kosha.

Manomaya Kosha

Next is the level of living energy, the mental sheath, the Manomaya kosha or the 'covering of mind', the emotional body or what Vedanta calls the mind. This level of mental activity is commonly captured in the Sanskrit term manas (from the verbal root man, meaning "to think"). The manas is the sensory-motor mind, which thrives on the material gathered from the senses of hearing, touch, sight, taste, and smell. This sheath deals with the emotional, mental or perceptual part of the body, which comprises not just the mind, but also the organs within the body. Its functions relate to perceptual organization. It is the level that receives impulses from the external world through the senses, organizes the sensory data, processes thoughts, emotions, and meaningful patterns, influences the Prana kosha, and channels the ways one thinks. The Manomaya kosha is where thinking and doubting occurs. This is the conceiving intellect, made up of thoughts that interpret the patterns of activity that the senses perceive. Thus interpreted, these patterns are conceived as meaningful information, about an intelligible world. This kosha is where all thoughts originate: the doubts, the anger, the lust, the exhilaration, the depression and the delusion. This kosha represents inventive, critical thought: the making of novel connections, the combination of ideas.

Vijnanamaya Kosha

Identified with "higher" mental functions, often expressed in the term buddhi that consists of the intellect (thoughts), the ego (sense of individuality), and the chitta (informational memory), Vijnanamaya kosha, represents not only 'cognition' but also 'intellect' and 'wisdom.' Vijnana means "certain knowledge"; it includes the three mental activities of feeling, willing, and knowing. It also represents the mind, skill and all the intelligence behind human work. This sheath represents the intelligence or the consciousness that is the discriminative part of the mind underneath the processing, thinking aspect of mind. It knows, decides, judges, and discriminates. This is the organ of philosophical thought and metaphysical intuition. It is also the seat of the human will, by which one orients life toward either unreflective bodily experience or enhanced awareness and spiritual realization. The Manomaya and Vijnanamaya sheaths together constitute what is called the mind. First there is Manomaya thought, which is on a level above mere physical or emotional reaction, but is still based on complex manipulations of ideas derived from the physical world. Manomaya kosha is the gross level of mind comprising emotions, thoughts, and different types of feelings and has no capacity to discriminate between right and wrong deeds according to situations. The Vijnanamaya kosha governs the gross mind to take appropriate decisions with knowledge that has been accrued through various means. It is based on taking intuitions from the upper realms and using them to guide one's feelings and actions. In the first, the reflexes are in control; in the second, one's higher intuitions are in control.

Anandamaya Kosha:

Bliss is not a static feeling but rather dynamic and unlimited, flowing uninterruptedly out of Consciousness. Anandamaya kosha, the blissful sheath, is the most interior of the kosha, the first of the koshas surrounding the Atman, the eternal center of consciousness. When one transcends all the previous layers, one is in bliss with life. Bliss is the highest dimension of our existence. It is a state of being in which one can detach oneself from the emotions and live in perfect health of body and mind. This is the most harmonious state of mind possible, associated with states of ecstasy and rapture. Many Yoga devotees, many Yoga masters and the Buddha and other spiritual masters lived this existence in a state of bliss and acquired much knowledge through the power of meditation and dis-identification with the external self. This is a state characterized by positive feeling, which is not dependent on any object or events of external reality. Thus, the "experience of ananda, bliss, is a qualitatively different sense of positive state and well being from that is associated with other sheaths, koshas. Also called the Causal layer and considered as the deepest and most subtle in human personality, this layer forms the subtlest of sheaths . It is the co-coordinating layer of personality, with the word ananda or 'happiness' being used in the sense of 'harmony', 'integration', and complete satisfaction or fulfillment, the experience one has when completely free from any kind of stress or disharmony, conflicts or compulsions, needs, drives, or anxieties.

This kosha is not bound by either time or space. This is the body one enters whenever a desire is fulfilled and also in the thought-free state characteristic of nirvikalpa samadhi and, more familiarly, deep sleep. When used by Buddhists and the Vedic sages who preceded them, bliss (Ananda) is the vibrancy of creation, the underlying dynamism that enters the world as vitality, desire, ecstasy, and joy.

Anandamaya kosha can be described as the transcendental body, and the experience of this state is sometimes taken as the highest ascent of mystical experience, an experience of total transcendence or the blissful body.

Ananda is the natural innate state of the conscious being and can remain elusive unless one follows righteous actions with the right attitudes as dictated by conscience and discriminative faculty.

It is Anandamaya kosha that dissolves the veil of the mind leading to ecstasy, bliss and what Maslow calls "integrated creativity" from which "comes the great work of art, or philosophy or science" (Maslow, 1968, p. 142). These qualities correspond to the higher ranks in Maslow's hierarchy of needs, low levels of narcissism, and a high degree of personal integration. It is when in Anandamaya state that one connects to consciousness resulting in transcendental awareness, transcending the ordinary limits of the physical world and experiencing spiritual states of consciousness.

Conclusion:

So by practicing Panch Kosh vivek, we can get an overall view of our true self. Our body identification gives way to identification of our whole self and not parts thereof. We rightly say that body , mind and intellect are only my parts and function because of me. Death of body is not my death. Any damage to my ornaments is not damage to the substrate of gold. A new ornament would manifest out of the core gold.

This knowledge is helpful for a seeker as it puts things in perspective. However, one has to follow a structured approach to achieve this goal of blissful experience.

Rishi Patanjali through his famous Yoga Sutra has provided the steps necessary towards self realization using Ashtanga Yoga (Eight Limbed Yoga). We shall try to understand the key facets of this Yoga Sutra in the next chapter.

Online Resources:

Cycle of reincarnation

https://youtu.be/kkMbbrOR1qw?si=tGcRkK_6vy0DFwF

The Secret of the Five Sheaths by Swami Sarvapriyananda

https://youtu.be/rPtHCCT1SZM?si=iuM0AnUWHgf6VS0H

CHAPTER EIGHT

PATANJALI'S YOGA SUTRAS

Hari Om
(Asato Ma Sad Gamaya, Tamaso Ma Jyotir Gamaya, Mrityor Ma
Amritam Gamaya)
Lead us from ignorance to truth, Lead us from darkness to light,
Lead us from death to deathlessness.
- Brihadaranyaka Upanishad

In the previous chapter using the Panch Kosh vivek method, an attempt was made to unbundle our personality; starting from the physical body as we move inward our ultimate goal is to get a glimpse of true spiritual self.

What is the motivation for undertaking this journey?

Those of us interested to rise above pains and sorrow by acquiring a detached perspective towards life events could be the possible candidates.

There are alternatives to this journey. We may seek support of a personal God to help us tide over difficult patches by sincere devotion and accept whatever we face in life as His will. This would constitute Bhakti yoga approach. All major religions of the world ; be it Christianity, Islam or Hindu, seem to have a construct about an all powerful God with various attributes that are super human and provide the devotee a sense of security as one goes through life. For life after death also many concepts like Paradise, Jannat and Swarg exist that tend to modulate our behavior while alive.

However, Vedic approach to the mystery of life has a slightly different approach. It propounds that the ultimate cause of this universe is an impersonal, Conscious being called Brahman. It goes on to suggest that the individual being (Jiva) at one's core is either a small part or whole of Brahman. However, because of ignorance (Avidya), Jiva is unable to relate with this Brahman. This individual being (Jiva) faces happiness and sorrows in present life based on the past life samskaras.

The concepts of rebirth and theory of Karma is based on the four Vedas, a body of knowledge believed to be manifested by the Creator of this world to ancient Rishis (seekers of knowledge) during their spiritual quest.

Knowledge portions (Jnana Kand) of the four Vedas also called Upanishads, have deep insights about the nature of this world and its Creator.

Brahma Sutras, attributed to Sage Ved Vyas, is an attempt to cull out this sacred wisdom. The Brahma Sutras later became basis for very structured commentaries by other Rishis and gave birth to Samkhya philosophy that started with a concept of duality i.e. Brahman and Jiva being independent entities. Rishi Kapila, its proponent, stipulates eternal existence of sentient Soul (Brahman, or Purusha) and insentient Nature (Prakriti or Maya). All worldly creations are the result of a relationship established between these two.

While various offshoots of Brahma Sutras like Samkhya, Advaita or Vishisht Advaita are philosophical constructs that differ from each other in certain nuances, they continue to coexist with healthy debate to know the ultimate reality.

These are open systems and unlike various religions including Hindu Sanatan Dharma, do not consider personal God as the center feature. While religions are useful in managing societies and impose some discipline in the behavior of masses, at times, religions and cults emanating from them are known to be the cause of conflict. Faith is the central theme of religions and cults. It tends to bring conformist tendencies in the practitioner and may not appeal to rationality of many, particularly with the spread of scientific temper in current world societies.

The vedantic systems being open ended and suggesting an impersonal Creator of this world may be more to the liking of scientific temper. Uptake of spirituality in modern times is an indication of its growing popularity.

While describing the concept of rebirth as per Hindu scriptures, we had indicated the possibility of one realizing one's true self by following a structured path under guidance of a suitable person who has already undertaken this journey of Self realization and is available in physical form as his destined karmas (Prarabdha Karma) are still not exhausted so he cannot drop his gross physical body.

In Hindu thoughts , Patanjali yoga sutra is considered to be one structured approach towards realization of our true self. As a departure from the philosophical theories, it attempts to provide us a stage by stage blueprint for action.

No affiliation with any religion is necessary. Any person interested in this self discovery journey can get on board. However, there are essential steps that need to be taken. These are universal in nature and there cannot be any short cut.

According to Patanjali, the key goal of the journey is to still (calm down) our mental tendencies (Chitta Vrati) . When our highest mind layer called 'Chitta' is perfectly still with no tendencies perturbing it, one gets a realization of one's true self.

It is akin to viewing the image of a full moon in the calm water of a lake. The lake is like our Chitta and viewing the moon is the process of self realization.

This process of stilling or calming the Chitta and viewing our true self can only be understood by undertaking the journey.

As our mental faculties are already dropped on the way towards the final goal of self realization (Samadhi), it is impossible to describe it by a realized seeker. Words fail him; so to say. It can only be alluded to and hence guidance by a suitable teacher is recommended.

However, it is a very personal , life changing experience that alters our self image permanently and one goes through life after this self realization, with equanimity under pleasure and pain.

The Yoga Sutras of Patanjali provide a comprehensive blueprint for self-realization and spiritual enlightenment. The main purpose of yoga is to learn to control our mind and not be controlled by our thoughts. Through yoga we learn to dissociate from our thoughts.

The teachings and practices of the Yoga Sutras are based on three principles:

1) Suffering is not caused by forces outside of us but by our faulty and limited perception of life and of who we are. Suffering is not caused by the situation, but by our thoughts about the situation.

2) The unwavering peace we seek is realized by experiencing the unlimited and eternal peace that is our true identity. Though hidden by our ignorance, it exists within us, waiting to be revealed. Peace exists within us.

3) Peace and self-realization is attained by mastering the mind. Only a single-pointed, calm mind can reveal the true self.

There are 196 sutras (aphorisms) presented in four chapters (or padas). Each pada emphasizes a different aspect of the science of yoga.

Patanjali divided his Yoga Sutras into 4 chapters or books (Sanskrit pada), containing in all 196 aphorisms (Sutras), divided as follows:

Pada 1: Concentration (Samadhi Pada)

Pada 2: Practice (Sadhana Pada)

Pada 3: Experiences (Vibhuti Pada)

Pada 4: Absolute Freedom (Kaivalya Pada)

The Eight Limbs of Yoga (Ashtanga Yoga):

The Yoga Sutras outline an eight-fold path known as Ashtanga Yoga, which serves as a systematic approach to self-realization. Figure 1 describes the hierarchy of these limbs. The end objective of Samadhi or Self Realization is achieved only after the remaining seven underlying stages are firmly established. Yama and Niyam are the foundational attributes and are at the same level. Similarly Asan and Pranayama are shown at same level as they relate to our body.

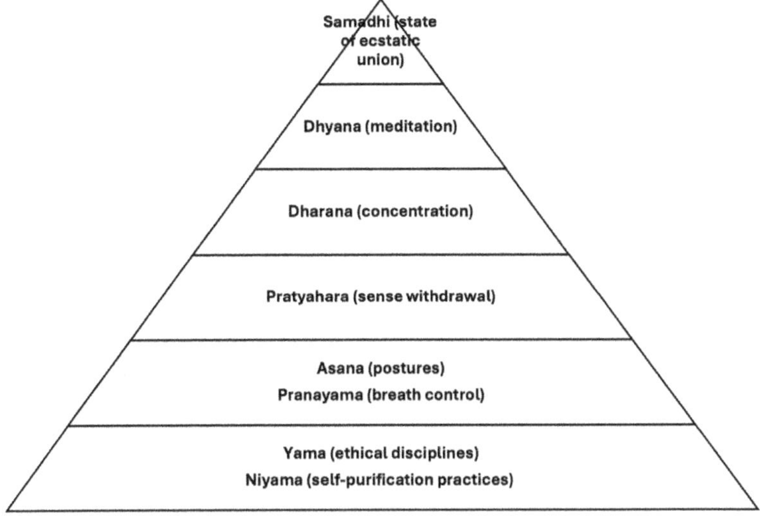

Figure 1: Hierarchy of Eight Limbs of Yoga

These eight limbs are as given below:
Yama (ethical disciplines)

- Ahimsa (non-violence)
- Satya (truthfulness)
- Asteya (non-stealing)
- Brahmacharya (moderation of the senses/right use of energy)
- Aparigraha (non-greed)

Niyama (self-purification practices)

- Saucha (cleanliness) Saucha can be translated as 'cleanliness', but it doesn't just mean physical cleanliness
- Santosha (contentment)
- Tapas (discipline)

- Svadhyaya (self study)
- Isvara Pranidhana (surrendering to a higher power)

Asana (postures)
Pranayama (breath control)
Pratyahara (sense withdrawal)
Dharana (concentration)
Dhyana (meditation)
Samadhi (state of ecstatic union)
Stilling the Modifications of the Mind:
A central tenet of the Yoga Sutras is that the goal is to stop (still) the fluctuations of the mind (chitta vritti nirodhah). By quieting the constant chatter and distractions of the mind, one can experience the true nature of the Self or Purusha.

The Practice of Kriya Yoga:
Patanjali outlines a three-part process called Kriya Yoga, which consists of tapas (austerity/discipline), svadhyaya (self-study), and Ishvara pranidhana (surrender to the Divine). This practice purifies the body, mind, and spirit, preparing the individual for self-realization.

The Contemplation of Ishvara (The Lord):
The Yoga Sutras recommend the contemplation of Ishvara, or the Lord, as a means to attain the highest form of Samadhi (union). This can be achieved through devotion, repetition of sacred words (mantras), or contemplation on the qualities of the Divine.

The Removal of Afflictions (Kleshas):
Patanjali identifies five afflictions (kleshas) that hinder self-realization: ignorance (avidya), egoism (asmita), attachment (raga), aversion (dvesha), and clinging to life (abhinivesha). The Yoga Sutras provide methods to overcome these obstacles.

The Development of Discriminative Discernment (Viveka Khyati):
Viveka Khyati, or discriminative discernment, is the ability to distinguish between the eternal Purusha (Self) and the temporary Prakriti (material world). This insight is essential for self-

realization.

By systematically following the eight limbs, practicing Kriya Yoga, contemplating the Divine, removing afflictions, and developing discriminative discernment, the Yoga Sutras of Patanjali provide a comprehensive framework for attaining the ultimate goal of self-realization and union with the Divine.

It may be observed that the first five limbs starting from Yama/Niyamas upto Pratyahara (sense withdrawal)or the Kriya yoga are focussing on external part of the seeker's personality.However, without this tuning of external dimension of our personality the final two stages leading to Samadhi (Self Realization) are impossible.

Thus a holistic approach is necessary.By following the eight limbs of yoga, individuals synchronize their mind, body, and soul. Each limb builds upon the others, creating a holistic approach to self-realization and inner harmony. Through ethical conduct, physical postures, breath control, and meditation, practitioners can deepen their spiritual connection, quiet the mind, and experience profound states of awareness and bliss.

Certain practical suggestions for practicing Yamas and Niyamas in our daily life are suggested below.

1. Yamas (Ethical Guidelines):

- Non-Violence (Ahimsa):

- In daily life, a seeker can practice ahimsa by avoiding harm to others physically, emotionally, or verbally.

- Real-world example: Choosing not to engage in gossip or spreading rumours about someone.

- Truthfulness (Satya):

- Seekers can practice satya by being honest and transparent.

- Real-world example: When asked about their opinion, a seeker refrains from exaggerating or distorting the truth.

- Non-Stealing (Asteya):

- Asteya involves not taking what doesn't belong to us.

- Real-world example: A seeker respects intellectual property rights and avoids piracy or plagiarism.

- Continence (Brahmacharya):
- Brahmacharya is about moderation and channeling energy appropriately.
- Real-world example: A seeker practices moderation in food, entertainment, and relationships.
- Non-Greed (Aparigraha):
- Aparigraha encourages detachment from material possessions.
- Real-world example: A seeker donates unused items to charity rather than hoarding them.

2. Niyamas(Personal Observances):
- Cleanliness (Saucha):
- Saucha involves physical and mental purity.
- Real-world example: A seeker maintains a clean living space and practices hygiene.
- Contentment (Santosha):
- Santosha is about finding contentment regardless of external circumstances.
- Real-world example: A seeker appreciates what they have instead of constantly desiring more.
- Self-Discipline (Tapas):
- Tapas refers to inner strength and willpower.
- Real-world example: A seeker wakes up early for meditation even when tempted to sleep in.
- Self-Study (Svadhyaya):
- Svadhyaya involves introspection and self-reflection.
- Real-world example: A seeker regularly journals their thoughts and emotions.
- Devotion to a Higher Power (Ishvara Pranidhana):
- Ishvara pranidhana is surrendering to a divine force.
- Real-world example: A seeker practices gratitude and acknowledges a higher purpose in life.

3. Integration into Daily Life:
- Seekers can integrate these principles into their routines:
- Morning Practice: Begin the day with meditation, expressing gratitude, and setting intentions.

- Mindful Actions: Throughout the day, practice mindfulness in interactions, speech, and actions.

- Evening Reflection: Reflect on how well you embodied the yamas and niyamas during the day.

Remember that these ethical guidelines and personal observances are not rigid rules but flexible principles. Seekers adapt them to their unique circumstances, always striving for self-improvement and inner growth.

How is Samadhi reached?

It may be surprising to many of us but we all have been experiencing a state of Samadhi on a daily basis during dreamless deep sleep.

Our mind and senses are suspended in deep sleep and the only observer of that state is our true self. However, the absence of mind during this process inhibits us from recalling details of that state.

We have a vague feeling of having enjoyed that state after we wake up and as we all know, sleep is essential for our continued wellbeing.

So we connect with our true self on a regular basis. The fact of the matter is that our true conscious self is the ONLY observer of all our worldly experiences.

Our mind , senses and body are just plain inert matter being made to appear live by the power of the conscious self.

During Samadhi we attempt a voluntary reunion with this true self by process of meditation. Thus meditation is essential for realizing our true self.

Even in Bhakti (Devotion) yoga the ultimate union with Divine is considered to be a meditative surrender of our limited self to the Divine within.

Samadhi is actually a fourth state also called Turiya (numeral 4 in Sanskrit) in which we enter while fully awake by a process of stilling the perturbations in our mind. The other three are our waking, dream and deep sleep states.

Samadhi is deemed to have taken place when our mind is completely still, much like the placid water of a clean lake, reflecting the Moon from the night sky. The Moon is our true self.

There is no hard boundary separating the two phases viz. Sadhna and Samadhi. The eight limbs of Ashtanga Yoga consists of the first preparatory steps connected with ourselves and the environment we live in.

They are preparations to ensure that we progress smoothly through Dharna (Concentration) and Dhyan (Meditation). Effective meditation increases our possibility to get a glimpse of divinity within. Figure 2 attempts to capture this process towards self-realization.

This process entails a very high proportion of actual practice. Like Cycling, Swimming or Dancing can not be learnt by watching YouTube videos alone and actual practice is necessary, same is the case with Yoga.

This spiritual journey of a seeker can be understood by a metaphor of an Aircraft getting airborne.

Preparatory Sadhna is akin to the ground crew working on it to ensure it's airworthiness. The process of taxiing to the runway takeoff point is like Dharna.

The takeoff run with full throttle is equivalent to Dhyan. Only when an aircraft reaches a critical speed can it get unstuck from the runway and get airborne. Similarly the Dhyan has to be firm to reach the Samadhi stage.

Once airborne aircraft gets over it's earlier limitations of not being able to travel across unpaved lands, rivers or mountains. Similarly a seeker in Samadhi stage transcends the earlier limitation of his mind and experiences a new found freedom or liberation.

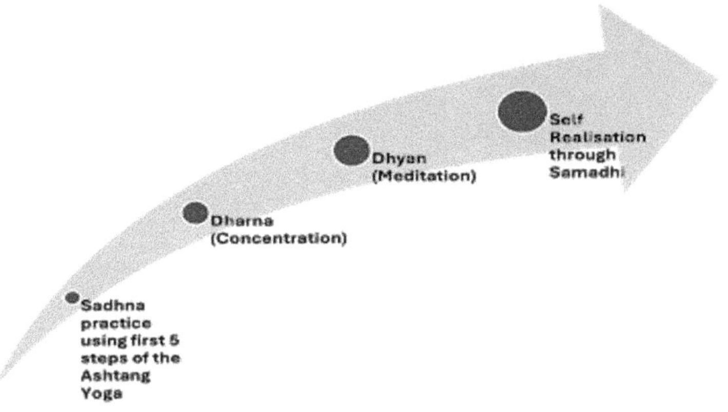

Figure 2: Process towards Self-Realisation

It is observed that a seeker may have apprehension in following the preparatory phase of observance of five Yamas, five Niyamas, stabilizing of Asan (Physical Exercises to strengthen the body), Pranayama (Breathing Exercises) and Pratyahara (Withdrawal of senses from world objects).

It is recommended that a seeker may motivate oneself to take the initial baby steps on this path, by appreciation of the immense value that the glimpse of the divine within provides them at the end of the long tunnel of spiritual Sadhna.

Another factor that inhibits us on this path is the fear of the unknown. The very idea of losing our existing concept of self to a very nebulous construct of divine self and consequences of this transformation on our 'business as usual' life, acts as a damper.

However, this fear is totally unfounded. A realized person is able to lead life with much better control on their interactions with the world around them. Many insecurities and dissipation of our energies in useless pursuits give way to a more holistic approach to life and our relations with others including our immediate family and friends become better.

Having allayed these fears of the seeker, we may take a brief look at the actual process. Though this journey is a personal quest, the need of a teacher/guide (Guru) to guide is emphasized. Even for the Sadhna phase, the role of a suitable guide or a course of instruction is highly recommended.

Like in any discipline, the need to have our concepts clarified through self-study (Svadhyaya) and reflection (Manan) is essential to get the critical mass of detachment (Vairagya) from worldly indulgences. Future posts would attempt to provide relevant information as considered necessary for a seeker.

Yoga Sutra, is one of the most detailed maps of higher consciousness; it deals primarily with the nature of mind, and with how the mind is transformed through different stages of samadhi (higher consciousness) until the liberated state, or kaivalya, finally appears.

Samadhi Pada is the opening chapter of Patanjali's Yog-Darshan or Yoga Sutras. It consists of 51 sutras that delve into the concept of enlightenment and the path to self-realization.

The term "samadhi" refers to a state of deep concentration, meditation, and absorption where the individual's consciousness merges with the object of focus. In this state, the sense of separation between the observer and the observed dissolves, leading to profound inner realization.

Purpose of Yoga According to Samadhi Pada:

Patanjali explains that the purpose of yoga is to quiet the fluctuations of the mind, known as "vrittis." These mental fluctuations are the source of restlessness, distractions, and suffering.

By practicing yoga, one aims to still these mental fluctuations and experience the true nature of the self beyond the conditioned mind.

Chitta-Vritti-Nirodha: Stilling the Mind:

• A central concept in Samadhi Pada is "chitta-vritti-nirodha," which refers to the stilling or calming of the mind-stuff (chitta).

- Through various yogic practices, the seeker learns to quiet the mind, allowing it to settle into a state of stillness and clarity.

Overcoming Obstacles:

- The chapter discusses obstacles and distractions that hinder the attainment of samadhi. These include desires, attachments, aversions, and other mental disturbances.

- Patanjali presents a path for overcoming these obstacles through the practice of "abstinences" (yamas) and "observances" (niyamas).

Types of Samadhi:

1. Savikalpa Samadhi:

o In this state, the mind is concentrated and still, but the merger with the object of focus is not yet complete.

o The practitioner experiences a deep meditative absorption, but there is still a subtle sense of duality.

2. Nirvikalpa Samadhi:

o This is the highest state of samadhi.

o The mind is fully absorbed and merged with the object of focus, leading to a complete dissolution of the sense of self.

o In Nirvikalpa Samadhi, the seeker experiences oneness and unity with the divine or the true self.

Importance of Samadhi:

- Samadhi is considered the crowning achievement of yogic practice. It represents the apex of the yogic journey, where the seeker transcends ordinary consciousness and enters a state of profound realization.

- Attaining samadhi is crucial for achieving liberation (moksha) and self-realization.

In summary, Samadhi Pada establishes the fundamental principles of yoga, emphasizing the quieting of the mind and the practice of samadhi as a means to realize the true self. It invites seekers to explore the depths of their consciousness and experience the ultimate union with existence.

In next chapter 9, we present key insights from three basic explanatory texts of vedanta namely, Tattva Bodha, Atma Bodha and Vivekchudamai.

A practical guide to this important topic of Samadhi as a resource, a link to YouTube videos play list of 11 videos by Swami Nikhilananda Saraswati is included in the resource section below.

These videos are a very authentic source of relevant information with examples from everyday life. Day 8 session has audio loss after about 20 minutes and viewer may switch to day 9 session without any noticeable discontinuity as in each session a recap of previous session is provided.

It is highly recommended that seeker may patiently listen to this set of 11 videos as convenient to get a grasp of this abstract topic. Practical experience of meditation would reinforce the key concepts brought out by a very accomplished speaker and immensely help the seeker in his journey.

Online Resources :

Who is Patanjalli? What is Yoga?

https://youtu.be/Bc5UHKO3wWc?si=G4NkgSeZqPlAFdrW

Patanjali Yoga Sutras by Swami Nikhilanand Sarswati- Day 1 | Samadhi Pada - Introduction Talk

https://youtu.be/vE94dzkgh2A?si=Rs0YJGY2hmttFGRm

Play list of 11 videos by Swami Nikhilananda Saraswati on Samadhi Pada

https://youtube.com/playlist?list= PLZx3LBhP9JWSFjlPqDxHNLdAXZQy-0JPT&si=Wmmz7y-sRIq1F75e

CHAPTER NINE

KEY CONCEPTS IN THREE EXPLANATORY TEXTS OF VEDANTA

Hari Om

In the previous chapter we have got a nodding acquaintance with the Patanjali Yoga sutras, that propose a practical approach for a seeker on the path of Spirituality.

One important aspect of preparatory phase is self study (Svadhyaya) of scriptures as it helps the seeker understand the context and strengthens Vairagya(detachment/ dispassion) and Vivek (discernment/discrimination) ; the two key ingredients that are crucial for meaningful progress in this discipline.

We attempt to learn about Tattva Bodha, Atma Bodha and Vivek Chudamani, the three important texts by Adi Shankaracharya, that cover a wide range of topics related to Advaita Vedanta philosophy.

Tattva Bodha- The Awakening to Reality

1. Introduction to Brahman:

- Definition and nature of Brahman (the ultimate reality)

- Attributes of Brahman (existence, consciousness, and bliss)

- Brahman as the cause of the universe

2. The Nature of the Self (Atman):
- Distinction between the Self and the body, mind, and senses
- The Self as the knower, the subject of knowledge
- The Self as the witness consciousness
3. The Identity of Brahman and the Self:
- The doctrine of non-duality (Advaita)
- The identity of the individual Self (Jivatman) with the Supreme Self (Paramatman)
- The concept of "Tat Tvam Asi" (That Thou Art)
4. The Ignorance (Avidya) and Its Effects:
- Avidya as the root cause of bondage and suffering
- The concept of Maya (the world as an appearance)
- The effects of Avidya (creation, sustenance, and dissolution of the universe)
5. The Path to Self-Realization:
- The means of knowledge (Jnana Yoga)
- The importance of discrimination (Viveka)
- The practice of dispassion (Vairagya)
6. The Study of the Scriptures:
- The role of the Vedas, Upanishads, and other sacred texts
- The importance of a qualified teacher (Guru)
- The process of self-inquiry (Atma Vichara)
7. The Four-fold Means of Knowledge:
- Discrimination between the real and the unreal (Nitya-Anitya Vastu Viveka)
- Renunciation of the fruits of action (Iha-Amutra Phala Bhoga Viraga)
- The six virtues (Shama, Dama, Uparati, Titiksha, Samadhi, and Shraddha)
- The desire for liberation (Mumukshutva)
8. The Stages of Self-Realization:
- The preparatory stage (Shravana)
- The stage of reflection (Manana)
- The stage of direct realization (Nididhyasana)
9. The State of Liberation (Moksha):

- The nature of liberation

- The characteristics of a liberated being (Jivanmukta)

- The attainment of bliss and freedom from the cycle of birth and death

Atma Bodha- Knowledge of Self

Atma Bodh, also known as the Knowledge of the Self, is a renowned work by the great Indian philosopher and spiritual teacher, Adi Shankaracharya (788-820 CE).

This text is considered a foundational work in the Advaita Vedanta tradition, which emphasizes the non-dual nature of reality and the ultimate oneness of the individual self (Atman) with the universal Brahman.

According to Atma Bodha, we have three distinct bodies (Sareeras) namely, Sthoola (Gross), Sookshma (Subtle) and Karana(Causal).

We have studied Panch Kosha Vivek in earlier chapter and our gross body is equivalent to Annamaya Kosha in that construct. Figure 1 below is reproduced to refresh our memory.

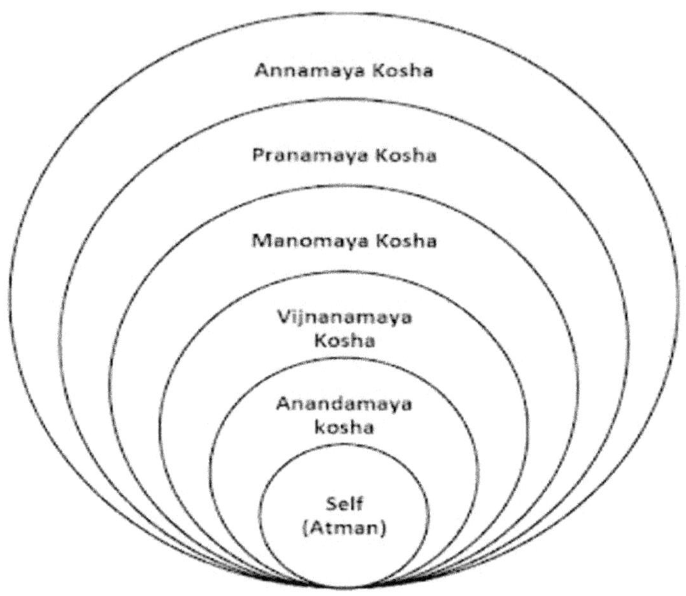

Fig 1 : The pictorial view of five Sheaths that constitute our personality

Subtle body, the Sookshma Sareera, is a combination of seventeen ingredients, five pranas, ten organs (5 sense organs and 5 organs of action), mind and Intellect, the instruments with which we experience pain and pleasure. It is thus composed of three koshas namely, Pranamaya, Manomaya and Vijnanamaya koshas as indicated in Figure 1 .

Causal body, the Karan Sareera, is also called Avidya (Ignorance) and is the cause of both gross and subtle bodies.

Anandmaya Kosha of Panch Kosha viveka corresponds to the Causal body. Based on our past karmas and impressions stored in the Causal body we get appropriate subtle and gross bodies.

The Sthoola Sareera, gross body, is the one that gets old, diseased and dies. Sookshma Sareera leaves the gross body at the time of death and gets rebirth.

It is not Atma that gets rebirth, according to Advaita doctrine. Atma is nothing but a form of Paramatma, the Brahman. It manifests itself in Sookshma Sareera and gets involved in the ties of human relations and gets elations and sorrows.

It also does various Karmas both good and bad. The results of those Karmas follow and the Sookshma Sareera gets the rewards called good births and punishments called mean births.

This process of rebirth stops only if in any birth this Sookshma Sareera gets out of Maya and understands the Atma in its body and gives up all worldly attachments and starts leading a life that befits Paramatma.

Then it will join Paramatma which is called Moksha. Till it is attained this worldly pleasures and sorrows will be hunting it in every birth.

Avidya (ignorance), has no beginning and is also quite difficult to define. As indicated above, it is also called Karana Sareera (Causal Body).

So every living body has three forms of sareera viz., Sthoola (gross body), Sookshma (subtle body) and Karana (causal body).

The gross body and subtle body are products of Avidya and therefore Avidya is called the causal body.

Atma is none of these three. It is the witness to the three bodies and never gets identified with them.

Atma or self luminous consciousness, illuminates the activities of the gross and subtle bodies. It is, however, detached from all the three bodies. Because of ignorance we think and attribute all the qualities of the three Sareeras to Atma.

When covered by a blue cloth, a pure colourless crystal looks like a blue crystal. Similarly because of the union with the Five Koshas, the pure Atma appears to have borrowed their qualities upon itself.

Annamaya Kosha is the physical body.

Pranamaya Kosa is the one that has Five Pranas that breathes life into this physical body.

Manomaya Kosha is responsible for our twin feelings of happiness and sorrow. It controls our mind.

Vijnanamaya Kosha controls our intellect.

These three viz. Pranamaya, Manonaya and Vijnanamaya constitute the Sookshma Sareera (Subtle body).

The Anandamaya Kosha which belongs to our Karana Sareera and controls our emotions is, however ,not real Ananda. Real and eternal Ananda (bliss) belongs to Atma.

It is therefore stated clearly in Atma Bodha that none of the three sareeras (bodies) is Atma.

If I make a statement while awake that, " I had a peaceful sleep through the night except for a brief bad dream". Who could be making this statement ? In deep sleep the mind does not exist and in dream our gross body and senses of cognition are dormant, but our mind has taken form of the dreamer. Who is that entity that is able to witness all three states namely, waking, dream and deep sleep and thus make this statement that we are analysing?

Atma bodha makes us question our established notions and as a consequence of the process of contemplation/reflection, faulty notions are dropped and we get a glimpse of deeper aspects connected with our experience of self.

Key aspects covered in Atma Bodh:

1. The Nature of the Self (Atman):

Adi Shankara begins by establishing the existence of the Atman, the true Self, which is distinct from the physical body, the mind, and the intellect. He describes the Atman as eternal, conscious, and blissful, transcending the limitations of the material world.

2. The Illusion of Duality:

Shankara explains that the perception of duality, the separation between the individual self and the ultimate reality, is an illusion caused by ignorance (avidya). This ignorance veils the true nature of the Self and leads to the attachment to the external world and the cycle of birth and death.

3. The Path to Self-Realization:

Shankara outlines the path to self-realization, which involves the pursuit of knowledge (jnana), the practice of discrimination (viveka), and the cultivation of dispassion (vairagya). He emphasizes the importance of study, contemplation, and the guidance of a qualified teacher (guru) in attaining self-knowledge.

4. The Nature of Brahman:

Shankara elucidates the concept of Brahman, the ultimate reality that is infinite, eternal, and beyond all attributes. He establishes the non-dual relationship between the Atman and Brahman, stating that they are one and the same, a realization that leads to liberation (moksha).

Vivek Chudamani- Our Spiritual Compass

1. Introduction:

The text begins with an introduction that sets the stage for the dialogue between the teacher (Guru) and the disciple (Shishya). It emphasizes the importance of discriminating between the real and the unreal, which is the essence of the text.

2. The Qualifications for Self-Realization:

This section discusses the four essential qualifications (Sadhana Chatushtaya) required for attaining self-realization:

a) Discrimination between the real and the unreal (Nitya-Anitya Vastu Viveka)

b) Renunciation (Vairagya)

c) The six virtues (Shatsampat)- Tranquility (Shama), Self-control (Dama), Renunciation (Uparati), Forbearance (Titiksha), Faith (Shraddha), and Concentration (Samadhana) are the six virtues, the six treasures that one have to cultivate.

d) Intense desire for liberation (Mumukshutva).

3. The Nature of the Self:

Here, Shankaracharya explains the true nature of the Self (Atman) as distinct from the body, mind, and intellect. The Self is described as an eternal, pure consciousness, and the ultimate reality (Brahman).

4. The Path to Self-Realization:

This section outlines the various paths or means (Sadhanās) to attain self-realization, such as study of the scriptures (Sravana), contemplation (Manana), and meditation (Nididhyasana). It also discusses the obstacles (Vikshepa) that hinder progress on the path and how to overcome them.

5. The Attainment of Self-Realization:

This part describes the state of self-realization (Jivanmukti) and the experience of the highest bliss (Ananda) that results from the realization of one's true nature as the Self.

6. The Means and Stages of Self-Realization:

Here, Shankaracharya elaborates on the different stages and means of self-realization, such as the practice of discrimination (Viveka), detachment (Vairagya), control of the mind (Sama), and concentration (Dama).

7. The Liberated State:

The final section discusses the state of complete liberation (Videhamukti) and the dissolution of individual existence into the ultimate reality (Brahman).

Online Resources:

Tattvabodh by Anubhavanand playlist of 7 videos.

https://youtube.com/playlist?list=
PLAF_c2xr3i8DKWyTTr0z_eRgB4IW-vvcS&si
=1oOdRqEEnw88rtQR

Swami Anubhavananda playlist of 17 videos on Atma bodha

https://youtube.com/playlist?list=
PLAF_c2xr3i8ASTRVs-8RTMMHQjg4OGnVv&si
=lyyAUp5X9EhByx2S

Swami Anubhavananda playlist of 9 videos on Vivekachoodamani

https://youtube.com/playlist?list=
PLAF_c2xr3i8CXOOELLFYLCa4NQOMUfdZg&si
=67ygD3fqSsLRP8bi

CHAPTER TEN

SYNTHESIS OF LEARNINGS FROM THREE ADVAITA VEDANTA TEXTS

Hari Om

In this chapter, we make an attempt to consolidate our learning so far from the earlier chapters. The insight generated by this exercise would help us plan a way forward for the seeker in a pragmatic and holistic manner.

If we try to recall the key concepts from the three highly regarded Advaita Vedanta texts, namely; Tattva Bodha, Atma Bodha and Vivek Chudamani an underlying key message that emerges is that the realization of our true nature as the eternal, blissful Atman (Self) that is one with Brahman (Ultimate Reality) is highest goal of human birth.

For ease of recall key points from all three are given in succeeding paragraphs.

Tattva Bodha (Knowledge of Truth) by Shankaracharya:

- Brahman is the sole reality, one without a second, eternal, conscious and infinite bliss. The world is an appearance, like a dream, on Brahman.

- The individual self (Jivatman) is really no different from Brahman, though it appears differentiated due to ignorance (Avidya).

- By attaining the knowledge "I am Brahman" through scripture and a qualified teacher, the illusion is destroyed, and one realizes identity with the Supreme Self.

Atma Bodha (Knowledge of Self) by Shankaracharya:

- The body, senses, mind and intellect together constitute the "not-Self." They are insentient and ever-changing.

- The Atman, our true Self, is the witnessing consciousness, eternal, all-pervading and unattached.

- To realize one's true nature, spiritual practices like discrimination between Self and not-Self, desirelessness, and control of mind/senses are recommended.

Viveka Chudamani (Crest-Jewel of Discrimination) by Shankaracharya:

- The world experienced is a superimposition (Adhyasa) on Brahman, like a snake appearing on a rope due to ignorance.

- Attachment to the body, fear, and egoism arise from ignorance of our true Self which is existence-consciousness-bliss (Sat-Chit-Ananda).

- Freedom comes from clear discrimination (Viveka) between the eternal Self and the not-Self, abandoning desires, and abiding as the ever-present witnessing consciousness.

The essence from these texts is: We are not the body, mind or intellect but the infinite Atman/Brahman. By inquiring "Who am I?" and gaining Self-knowledge from scripture and guru, the veil of ignorance dissolves. One then abides in the bliss of realizing one's true nature beyond all dualities and limitations.

These teachings guide the seeker to discriminate between the real and unreal, cultivate desirelessness and one-pointed focus to break free from bondage and suffering. The goal is the direct experience of one's divine Self and inseparable identity with the all-pervading Brahman - the lasting peace and freedom that is our very nature.

Several eminent spiritual masters and scholars have commented on the commonality of view presented in the texts Tattva Bodha, Atma Bodha, and Viveka Chudamani, highlighting their unified message of Advaita Vedanta or non-dualism. Here are some notable commentaries:

1. Swami Vivekananda:

Vivekananda considered these three works by Adi Shankaracharya as quintessential texts expounding the philosophy of Advaita Vedanta. In his words, "Tattva Bodha, Atma Bodha and Viveka Chudamani are the perfect foundations to understand the lofty principles of non-dualism or Advaita."

2. Ramana Maharshi:

The renowned sage Ramana Maharshi often recommended the study of these texts to seekers. He saw them as complementary works that systematically unveil the reality of the Self (Atman) and its identity with Brahman. Ramana highlighted their emphasis on Self-inquiry (Atma-Vichara) as the direct path to Self-realization.

3. Swami Chinmayananda:

This influential teacher has written extensive commentaries on all three texts. He saw them as forming "a graded, integrated course of study" leading the seeker from basic discrimination to the experience of non-dual Brahman. Chinmayananda praised their scientific approach and lucid expression of profound Vedantic concepts.

4. Swami Dayananda Saraswati:

A renowned Advaita scholar, Dayananda viewed these works as masterpieces that comprehensively unfold the teaching of "Tat Tvam Asi" (That Thou Art). He appreciated how they employ different methods - reasoning, analogies, and contemplative techniques - to reveal the same ultimate truth of non-duality.

5. Nisargadatta Maharaj:

Though from the Nath tradition, Nisargadatta frequently quoted from these Advaitic texts in his teachings. He saw them as expounding the highest knowledge - that the world is an appearance on the substratum of the single, non-dual Self or Brahman.

While using slightly different language and emphasis, eminent exponents across traditions have recognized Tattva Bodha, Atma Bodha and Viveka Chudamani as lucid, authoritative texts that provide a progressive, multi-faceted exposition of the core principles of Advaita Vedanta - the ultimate non-dualistic reality of Brahman/Atman and the means to realize it through knowledge and discrimination.

The teachings in Tattva Bodha, Atma Bodha and Viveka Chudamani share significant commonalities with the philosophy and practice outlined in Patanjali's Yoga Sutras.

Both systems ultimately point towards the realization of the true Self or Purusha, which is distinct from the mind-body complex.

In this chapter we attempt to map and integrate the key learnings from **three Advaitic texts covered in previous chapter with the sadhana process** suggested by Patanjali:

1. Discrimination between Purusha and Prakriti (Viveka):

Just as the Advaitic texts emphasize discriminating between the eternal Self (Atman) and the non-Self (body, mind, intellect), Patanjali's Yoga lays great importance on viveka - the ability to discern the conscious Purusha from unconscious Prakriti (nature/ manifested world).

2. Control of Chitta Vrittis (Mind Modifications):

The Advaitic teachings guide the seeker to go beyond the mind's conditioning and identifications. Patanjali's ashtanga yoga, especially the practices of ethical disciplines (yamas, niyamas), asanas, pranayama and pratyahara, serve to restrain and master the modifications of the mind (chitta vrittis).

3. Samadhi and Kaivalya (Liberation):

The ultimate goal in both Advaita Vedanta and Patanjali's Yoga is to abide in the true nature of the Self, free from all limitations. Samadhi, the state of unwavering concentration in Patanjali's system, aligns with the Advaitic vision of realizing one's identity with Brahman. Kaivalya or aloneness is akin to liberation from all dualities

4. Need for Shravana, Manana and Nididhyasana:

The Advaitic texts emphasize studying scripture (shravana), reasoning (manana) and constant contemplation (nididhyasana) to uproot ignorance. Similarly, the Yoga Sutras prescribe the practices of study (svādhyāya) and contemplation on the Lord (Ishvara pranidhana) as key aids on the spiritual journey.

5. Role of the Guru and Satsang:

Both the Advaitic and Yoga traditions underline the importance of a realized Guru's guidance to remove doubts and provide the ultimate teachings. Association with truth-seekers (satsang) is also highlighted as contributing to progress on the path.

Thus in essence, Patanjali's Raja Yoga can be seen as a comprehensive psycho-physical sadhana process to purify and prepare the mind-body vehicle for the ultimate realization of the Purusha or Atman, the changeless witnessing awareness expounded in the Advaitic texts.

The practices enable viveka (discrimination), vairagya (dispassion), removal of mental afflictions, and culminate in the direct experience of one's true nature, free from the notion of being the limited individual self.

The teachings in the Upanishads and other Hindu scriptures can be deeply understood and illuminated when viewed through the lens of the three seminal texts by Adi Shankaracharya - Tattva Bodha, Atma Bodha and Viveka Chudamani - as well as the Yoga Sutras of Patanjali. These later works systematize and elucidate the core principles found across the Upanishads and Vedic texts.

1. Non-duality of Brahman/Atman:

The Upanishadic mahavakyas like "Tat Tvam Asi" (That Thou Art) and "Aham Brahmasmi" (I am Brahman) point to the fundamental truth of non-dual Oneness between the individual self (Atman) and the cosmic Brahman. This is the central teaching expounded in Adi Shankara's Advaita treatises, providing a coherent philosophical framework.

2. Nature of the Self:

Descriptions in the Upanishads of the Atman as the eternal, consciousness principle distinct from the body-mind complex are systematically analyzed in Atma Bodha and Viveka Chudamani. These texts remove doubts about the true nature of the Self through reason and analogies.

3. World as Appearance:

The idea that the world is relatively unreal, a mere appearance (maya) on the substratum of Brahman is echoed in Tattva Bodha's analysis of the three states of experience - waking, dream and deep sleep. This aids in developing the discrimination between absolute and relative reality.

4. Means to Liberation:

The Upanishads recommend various spiritual practices like meditation, karma yoga, jnana yoga for Self-realization. Patanjali's Yoga Sutras synthesize these as the "yoga of action" (kriya yoga) and the "yoga of knowledge" (jnana yoga) as complementary means towards kaivalya (aloneness/liberation).

5. Guru and Shraddha:

Both the Upanishads and Advaitic texts like Viveka underscore the necessity of a realized Guru's guidance and shraddha (faith) in the teachings to remove doubts and ignorance obscuring Self-knowledge.

6. Ethical Disciplines:

The ethical injunctions (niyamas and yamas) outlined in Patanjali's ashtanga yoga system resonate with the virtues and codes of conduct emphasized across the Upanishads as prerequisites for spiritual evolution.

In essence, Adi Shankara's Prakarana Granthas and Patanjali's Yoga Darshana can be seen as coherent intellectual and practical maps that condense, synthesize and make accessible the profound wisdom of the ancient Upanishads and Vedic teachings on the path of Self-realization and spiritual illumination. They act as bridges to understand the spirit and essence of these venerable scriptures in a systematic manner.

Several modern eminent scholars and exponents of Vedanta have synthesized the learnings from the five primary sources - the Upanishads, Patanjali's Yoga Sutras, Tattva Bodha, Atma Bodha and

Viveka Chudamani - in their teachings and writings. We describe below, how some key figures have integrated insights from these texts:

1. Swami Vivekananda:

Vivekananda saw the Yoga Sutras as providing a practical psychological framework complementing the philosophical Advaita teachings of the Upanishads and Shankara's treatises. He harmonized them, highlighting Patanjali's Raja Yoga as the "psychological process" and Vedanta the "metaphysical backdrop" for attaining liberation.

2. Sri Aurobindo:

Aurobindo viewed the Upanishads and Shankara's works as expressing the highest spiritual knowledge and experience. He drew parallels between the yogic discipline described by Patanjali and the triad of shravana-manana-nididhyasana emphasized in Viveka Chudamani for Self-realization.

3. Swami Sivananda:

A prolific integrator of various Hindu spiritual traditions, Sivananda synthesized the teachings of Vedanta, Yoga, and Tantra philosophies. He recommended studying the Upanishads, Gita, Shankara's Prakarana works and Patanjali's Sutras together as a "gateway to the Absolute."

4. Swami Chinmayananda:

One of the foremost modern expositors of Advaita Vedanta, Chinmayananda's teachings and commentaries seamlessly wove in principles and practices from the Upanishads, Bhagavad Gita, Shankara's treatises and Patanjali's Yoga system. He presented them as complementary aids for "conscious spiritual living."

5. Swami Dayananda Saraswati:

An authority on Advaita philosophy, Dayananda harmonized the core teachings across texts like the Upanishads, Brahma Sutras, Viveka Chudamani and Yoga Sutras. He viewed the four primary spiritual practices (sadhana chatushtaya) mentioned across these works as an integrated approach for Self-knowledge.

6. Swami Satchidanandendra Saraswati:

This renowned Advaita scholar and teacher provided an insightful synthesis, highlighting how Shankara's works elucidate the Upanishadic teachings, while Patanjali's Yoga complemented Advaita by describing methods to prepare the mind for assimilating Self-knowledge.

The common thread is viewing the Upanishads as the loftiest scriptural source expounding non-dual Brahman, while the texts by Shankara and Patanjali provide an intellectual framework and practical disciplines to realize those ultimate truths in one's experience. By integrating these sources, modern scholars have presented Vedanta as a comprehensive knowledge system for spiritual illumination.

In the next and concluding chapter, using above insights we attempt to suggest a way forward for a seeker.

Resource:

Sri Swami Krishnananda's website offers a wealth of free online resources on Eastern and Western philosophies, Hinduism, mysticism, yoga, meditation and other topics related to spirituality. The website features writings, audios and videos of Swami Krishnananda, a renowned spiritual teacher and disciple of Sri Swami Sivananda.

Swami Krishnananda's teachings are insightful and profound, and they have the power to open up one's mind to different perspectives on life. This website is a great resource for anyone looking to explore the spiritual side of life and gain insight into way to attain knowledge of the Absolute.

It is highly recommended that a serious seeker spends good time to peruse the treasure of information available at the link below.

https://www.swami-krishnananda.org/

CHAPTER ELEVEN

WAY FORWARD

Hari Om

Using the insights provided in previous Chapters **Figure 1** below has been prepared. The synthesis of key learnings from five sources is intuitively performed by me and any alternate view is certainly possible. Moot point is to prioritize our activities and thus get strengths of all texts covered so far. Even if we follow one step at a time over say next six months , we may notice some changes in our mental energies and we may be motivated to take more baby steps. Don't worry. Spirituality is not a serious affair. It can be fun. Just get over the myths that surround this field and our fear of being derailed from our present vibrant social life.

Nothing is farther from truth. Only thing necessary is to try this alternative way of looking at life.

Key points from Basic Concepts from Hindu Scriptures

Karma Theory and Rebirth

Role of free will and possibility of Moksha

Guru's role as embodiment of knowledge

Five Koshas of personality and need to go beyond all five using discrimination to realize True Self

Key points from Patanjali Yoga Sutra

Eight Limbs of Yoga

Importance of Ethical and Disciplined living in Sadhna process

Faith in a Higher reality

Need for consistent practice without distraction to manifested special powers

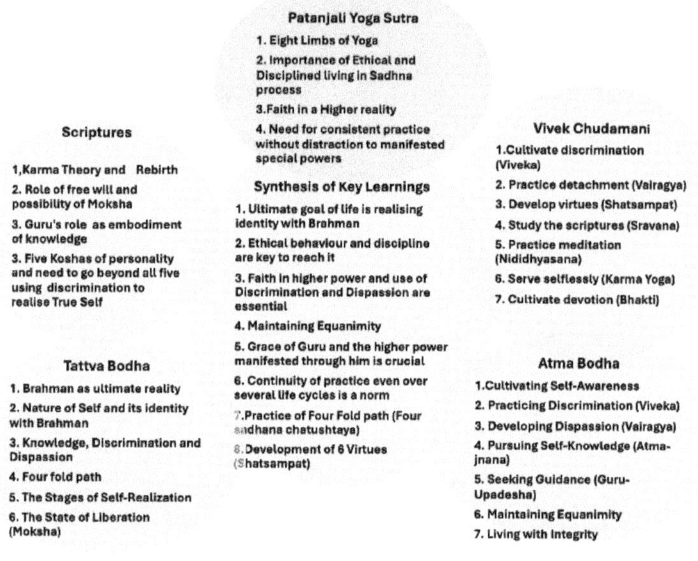

Figure 1: Synthesis of Learning from all previous chapters

Key points from Tattva Bodha

Brahman as ultimate reality

Nature of Self and its identity with Brahman

Knowledge, Discrimination and Dispassion

Four fold path (sadhana chatushtaya)-

(The pillars of Four fold path are Viveka (knowing the difference between self and no-self), vairagya (non-attachment), shatsampat* (attain a balance between mental and emotional in order to see things as they truly are), and mumukshutva (desire to achieve freedom from suffering).

*The details of shatsampat (six virtues) are given below to facilitate recall:

Sama (Mastery over the mind) ,

Dama (Control of the external senses),

Uparati (Observance of one's own dharma (duties)),

Titiksha (Endurance of opposites (heat and cold, pleasure and pain, etc)) ,

Sraddha (Reverential Faith in the words of the Scriptures and the Guru)

Samadhana (Focussing or single-pointedness of the mind).

Key points from Vivek Chudamani

Cultivate discrimination (Viveka)

Practice detachment (Vairagya)

Develop virtues (Shatsampat)

Study the scriptures (Sravana)

Practice meditation (Nididhyasana)

Serve selflessly (Karma Yoga)

Cultivate devotion (Bhakti)

Key points from Atma Bodha

Cultivating Self-Awareness

Practicing Discrimination (Viveka)

Developing Dispassion (Vairagya)

Pursuing Self-Knowledge (Atma-jnana)

Seeking Guidance (Guru-Upadesha)

Maintaining Equanimity

Living with Integrity

Synthesis of Key Learnings from the five sources listed above:

Ultimate goal of life is realising identity with Brahman

Ethical behaviour and discipline are key to reach it

Faith in higher power and use of Discrimination and Dispassion are essential

Maintaining Equanimity

Grace of Guru and the higher power manifested through him is crucial

Continuity of practice even over several life cycles is a norm

Practice of Four Fold path (Four sadhana chatushtaya)

Development of 6 Virtues (Shatsampat)

For a seeker treading the path of spirituality and Self-realization, the learnings from the five primary sources - the Upanishads, Patanjali's Yoga Sutras, Tattva Bodha, Atma Bodha and Viveka Chudamani - can possibly be embraced and integrated into daily life in the following ways:

1. Study and Reflection (Svadhyaya):

Regular study and contemplation of these sacred texts is the foundation. Setting aside daily time for svadhyaya - whether reading/listening to the original verses or commentaries - allows the teachings to penetrate the intellect.

2. Discrimination (Viveka):

Cultivating the ability to discriminate between the eternal Self and the impermanent non-Self, as emphasized in texts like Viveka Chudamani. Applying this viveka in every experience and constantly asking "Who am I?" in the midst of daily activities.

3. Ethical Disciplines (Yamas and Niyamas):

Imbibing and practicing the ethical restraints (yamas) and observances (niyamas) prescribed by Patanjali as prerequisites for spiritual growth. This lays the foundation for an effective sadhana.

4. Meditation and Contemplation:

Developing a daily practice of meditation as delineated in the Yoga Sutras and other texts. This can involve techniques like mantras, breath awareness, or the profound contemplation (nididhyasana) on profound Upanishadic statements like "I am Brahman."

5. Karma Yoga:

Performing all duties and actions in a spirit of selflessness and offering them to the Divine, as taught in texts like the Bhagavad Gita. This cultivates detachment and purifies the mind.

6. Seeking Guidance:

Regularly seeking the association (satsang) of realized guru figures who can remove doubts, provide instructions, and share realizations from their direct experience of the ultimate teachings.

7. Introspection and Self-Inquiry:

Setting aside time for regular self-inquiry and introspection in the manner of "Who am I?" as advocated by Adi Shankara to turn the mind inward from identification with objects.

8. Developing Qualities:

Consciously striving to inculcate the qualities conducive to Self-realization like humility, dispassion, perseverance, tranquility, self-control as outlined by various texts.

The key is to make spiritual sadhana an integrated and vibrant part of one's daily routine and not merely an event. With sincerity, commitment and the blessings of the guru's grace, steady and sustained practice of the teachings can ultimately culminate in the direct realization of the Self.

Swami Krishnananda of Divine Society in his book titled 'Spiritual Aspiration and Practice' has provided for a seeker very deep insights on the 3 components , Viveka, Vairagya and Shatsampat of four fold path(sadhana chatushtaya) and we reproduce it below for benefit of the reader.

"Viveka and vairagya are more of an intellectual and rationalistic nature, where you have to exercise your understanding and logical thinking much more than anything else.

But there is something else, which is called your feelings. "Whatever be the thing you say, I want this." This is what the heart of hearts will tell you. This heart has also to be disciplined in the same way as the intellect has to be disciplined through viveka and vairagya. Your heart is yourself. Your brain and intellect are not so connected with your existence as your feelings and heart.

"My heart is what I am." Now, this third requisite is called shad-sampat, the acquisition of six virtues. They are called sampat because they are actually treasures, very valuable things. The six virtues are sama, dama, uparati, titiksha, sraddha and samadhana.

Sama is a determination on your part to be always calm and quiet under any kind of condition, even aggressive conditions. It is very important. Hate does not cease by hate. Hate ceases by love. Reaction is not the way in which you have to conduct yourself towards an action. Two persons are necessary to quarrel, and you need not be a party in that. Restrain your mind with the help of the understanding that you have already exercised through viveka and vairagya.

Sama is the restraint of the internal organ, which is the mind, and dama is the restraint of the sense organs, the discipline of the organs outside. There is a distinction between the internal organ and the external organs. The internal organ, or the psyche proper, is called the antahkarana chatushtaya. Mano buddhi ahankara chitta: the mind that thinks, the buddhi or intellect that decides and determines, the ahankara that identifies everything with itself, and the chitta or memory that remembers past things; these are, broadly speaking, the functional aspects of the psyche.

Because they are four, they are called chatushtaya; and because it is an internal faculty, it is called , not external. That is the mind.

In Western psychology, the word 'mind' is used for all these four aspects. Sometimes they divide the mind into understanding, feeling and willingness. This is the limitation of psychology in Western thought. But there is much more about the mind than only this threefold classification. So much about the internal organ, about which we said sama is to be exercised.

Dama is the restraint of the five organs—the eyes, the ears and sensations of every kind. There are five senses of knowledge and five organs of action. The eyes have a passion to see certain things, and there is a passion for every sense organ. Passion is an uncontrollable desire. A desire that has overcome you and flooded you is called passion.

Desire is the beginning stage of an overwhelming, consuming longing. Desires insinuate themselves into you gradually, like diseases that crop up inside without your knowing that they are there and manifest themselves only afterwards through the body."

Embracing the comprehensive wisdom from the Upanishads, Shankara's Advaitic texts and Patanjali's Yoga system provides the seeker the philosophical depth, ethical and mental anchors, and yogic practices for the ultimate attainment of moksha - the state of freedom, peace and oneness

The spiritual journey is a very personal experience and progress would depend greatly on our circumstances in life. All of us are propelled by the past life Samskaras and the role of 'free will' is considered very crucial in changing the trajectory of our destiny towards liberation.

I hope our journey so far has helped us get a concise and clear understanding of what authentic texts prescribed in Vedanta and Hindu scriptures have to offer us. Knowledge acquisition along with contemplation on that knowledge is essential to spur us on Spiritual journey.

Like we plan our vacations and other business trips, we need to pay attention to our spiritual journey. I can only suggest by experience that one can have a very joyous and effective work life while allotting adequate time to Sadhna. As we go for physical activities to keep our body fit, Sadhna would have a holistic beneficial effect on our personality. We would enjoy our lives much better. Life would be a continuous celebration.

Resources:

This link is the immensely useful texts for a seeker. It takes you to Sri Swami Krishnananda's

website at The Divine Life Society. Do take a look.

https://www.swami-krishnananda.org/

Epilogue

Hari Om

All of us are born with a baggage of past life Samskaras (impressions) that seem to shape our life events. We may helplessly flow through life experiencing pleasures and pains and create new Samskaras (impressions) in turn that may determine our next births. However, our scriptures show us hope by pointing out '**free will**' bestowed on us as humans and the possibility to change our trajectory in this and future lives, if any.

Use of this free will is very well documented by Patanjali Yoga Sutras and they provide us a blueprint for action. There is no precondition in terms of gender, cast or creed. We need not necessarily have faith in a personal God. All that is necessary is willingness to accept the existence of a higher consciousness that seems to guide our lives and world around us.

Even an Atheist, with an open mind may embark on this journey with a scientific temper and willingness to experience the inner reality. In addition to the external world that we, in any case, experience during waking hours one may focus on inner world also through meditation process. Proposition that there is no reality other than the external material world is akin to throwing the baby with bath water. Our inner world exists, as perceived by all of us, through the sense of 'I' and we should be willing and courageous enough to explore the unknown.

I hope this book has helped you get a perspective on key issues connected with our inner personality. Just as by reading a detailed map or reading travel blogs we can not experience the joy of visiting a tourist destination, similarly reading scriptures and various philosophy texts can not be a suitable substitute for actual experience during meditation. Knowledge acquisition, along with contemplation on that knowledge, is essential to spur us on Spiritual journey.

We plan our vacations and other business trips by paying attention to details. Similar diligence is recommended to plan our spiritual journey. It is possible to achieve balance between our worldly duties and our spiritual quests. I may add that the spiritual pursuits actually take away other wasteful activities and we are able to contribute to our worldly roles with renewed vigor.

I can only suggest by experience that one can have a very joyous and effective work life while allotting adequate time to Sadhna (Spiritual Practice). We undertake physical training to maintain a healthy body. Similarly, Spiritual practice would have a lasting effect on our psyche that manifests in all round wellbeing and calmness in attitude towards life. Life is no more a reaction to events impacting on us but an unruffled passage that is not only good to us but to our family and friends. We become an asset to our society.

Happy journey!

Appendix A Panchadasi

Hari Om

Panchadasi is a comprehensive text of Advaita Vedanta written by Sri Swami Vidyaranya who is regarded highly as a great scholar in Advaita philosophy after Jagadguru Sri Sankaracharya.

It is a masterpiece in Vedanta philosophy and spiritual practice. It contains fifteen chapters, which is why it is called the Panchadasi.

The book by itself has no name; it is named after the number of chapters. Panchadasa is fifteen, and panchadasi is a work that contains fifteen chapters.

These fifteen chapters are classified into three sections of five chapters each.

Bhagavadgita, which was topic of last session 12, containing eighteen chapters, is also classifiable into three sections: the first six, the middle six, and the last six.

The first five chapters of the Panchadasi deal with **Existence, or Sat** in Sanskrit.

The second five chapters deal with **Consciousness, or Chit.**

The last five chapters deal with **Ananda, or Bliss.**

Therefore, the book as a whole is an exposition of Sat-Chit-Ananda—the nature of the Absolute expounded in minute detail in Vidyaranya's own novel way.

The three sections, each containing five chapters are listed below:

1. Viveka (Discrimination) Panchaka
2. Dipa (Lamp) Panchaka
3. Ananda (Bliss) Panchaka

1. Viveka Panchaka:

This section deals with the discrimination between the **real and the unreal.** It covers:

- The nature of reality **(Tattva Viveka)**
- The five sheaths or Koshas **(Pancha Kosha Viveka)**

- The distinction between the witness and the witnessed **(Sakshi Drik Viveka)**

- The nature of space **(Mahabhuta Viveka)**

- The non-dual reality **(Ananda Mimamsa)**

2. Dipa Panchaka:

This section uses the analogy of a lamp to illuminate various aspects of Vedantic teaching:

- The nature of **pure consciousness** (Chitradipa)

- The **reflected consciousness** (Kutastha Dipa)

- The **nature of Brahman** as existence-consciousness-bliss (Bhuma Dipa)

- The **identity of individual self and Brahman** (Advaita Dipa)

- The **unreality of duality** (Upadesa Sahasri Dipa)

3. Ananda Panchaka:

This final section explores the nature of bliss:

- The **bliss of Brahman** (Yogananda)

- The **bliss of self-realization** (Atmananda)

- The **bliss of non-duality** (Advaita Ananda)

- The **bliss of knowledge** (Vidyananda)

- The **nature of supreme bliss** (Vishaya Ananda)

Key Concepts in Panchadasi:

1. **Brahman**: The ultimate, non-dual reality.

2. **Maya**: The illusory power that creates the appearance of duality.

3. **Jiva**: The individual self, essentially identical with Brahman.

4. **Adhyasa**: Superimposition, the mistaken attribution of unreal qualities to the real.

5. **Sakshi**: The witness consciousness, unaffected by the changes in the mind.

Panchadasi: Detailed Content Analysis

I. Viveka (Discrimination) Panchaka

1. Tattva Viveka (Discrimination of Reality):

- Introduces the concept of Brahman as the ultimate reality

- Explains the difference between the absolute (paramarthika) and empirical (vyavaharika) levels of reality

- Discusses the nature of Maya and its role in creating the appearance of duality

2. Pancha Kosha Viveka (Discrimination of the Five Sheaths):

- Explores the five sheaths (koshas) that veil the true self:

a) Annamaya kosha (food sheath or physical body)

b) Pranamaya kosha (vital air sheath)

c) Manomaya kosha (mental sheath)

d) Vijnanamaya kosha (intellectual sheath)

e) Anandamaya kosha (bliss sheath)

- Explains how to discriminate between these sheaths and the true self (Atman)

3. Sakshi Drik Viveka (Discrimination of the Witness and the Seen):

- Introduces the concept of Sakshi (witness consciousness)

- Differentiates between the changing objects of perception and the unchanging witness

- Explains how the Sakshi is unaffected by the states of waking, dreaming, and deep sleep

4. Mahabhuta Viveka (Discrimination of the Great Elements):

- Analyzes the five great elements (earth, water, fire, air, and space)

- Shows how these elements are products of Maya

- Demonstrates that consciousness pervades and transcends all elements

5. Ananda Mimamsa (Investigation into Bliss):

- Explores the nature of bliss (ananda) as the essence of the self

- Distinguishes between relative happiness and absolute bliss

- Explains how bliss is not a state to be achieved but our true nature to be recognized

II. Dipa (Lamp) Panchaka

6. Chitradipa (The Lamp of Pure Consciousness):

- Describes consciousness as self-luminous, like a lamp

- Explains how consciousness illuminates all objects of experience

- Discusses the nature of pure consciousness as distinct from objects of consciousness

7. Kutastha Dipa (The Lamp of the Immutable Self):

- Explores the concept of Kutastha (the immutable self)
- Differentiates between the changing ego and the unchanging self
- Explains how the Kutastha is the substratum of all experience

8. Bhuma Dipa (The Lamp of the Infinite):

- Discusses the nature of Brahman as infinite and all-pervading
- Explains how the infinite appears as the finite due to Maya
- Explores the concepts of existence, consciousness, and bliss (sat-chit-ananda)

9. Advaita Dipa (The Lamp of Non-duality):

- Presents arguments for the non-dual nature of reality
- Refutes objections to non-dualism
- Explains how apparent duality arises from the non-dual Brahman

10. Upadesa Sahasri Dipa (The Lamp of a Thousand Teachings):

- Provides practical instructions for realizing non-dual reality
- Offers methods for overcoming obstacles in spiritual practice
- Emphasizes the importance of a qualified teacher (guru)

III. Ananda (Bliss) Panchaka

11. Yogananda (The Bliss of Yoga):

- Explores different types of yoga (karma, bhakti, raja, jnana)
- Explains how these paths lead to the experience of bliss
- Discusses the relationship between meditation and bliss

12. Atmananda (The Bliss of the Self):

- Describes the nature of self-knowledge
- Explains how self-knowledge leads to unshakeable happiness
- Differentiates between the bliss of the self and temporary pleasures

13. Advaita Ananda (The Bliss of Non-duality):

- Explores the ultimate bliss that comes from realizing non-dual reality

- Explains how this bliss is different from sensory pleasures
- Discusses the state of jivanmukti (liberation while living)

14. Vidyananda (The Bliss of Knowledge):

- Describes the joy that comes from spiritual knowledge
- Explains how knowledge removes ignorance and suffering
- Discusses the relationship between knowledge and bliss

15. Vishaya Ananda (The Bliss in Objects):

- Analyzes the nature of happiness derived from objects
- Shows how all happiness ultimately comes from the self
- Explains how to see the divine in all objects and experiences

Key Themes Running Through the Panchadasi:

1. The identity of Atman (individual self) and Brahman (universal self)

2. The illusory nature of the world (Maya) and how it veils our true nature

3. The importance of discrimination (viveka) between the real and the unreal

4. The nature of consciousness as self-luminous and all-pervading

5. The concept of witness consciousness (Sakshi) as our true nature

6. The five sheaths (koshas) that seemingly cover the self

7. The nature of bliss (ananda) as our essential nature

8. The path to self-realization through knowledge and meditation

9. The state of liberation (moksha) and its characteristics

The Panchadasi systematically builds its arguments, starting from the nature of reality and the self, moving through the analysis of experience and consciousness, and culminating in the exploration of bliss and liberation. It uses various analogies, logical arguments, and references to scriptures to convey its teachings, making it a comprehensive text for those seeking to understand Advaita Vedanta philosophy.

Modern Exponents and Their Interpretations of Panchdasi:

1. Swami Chinmayananda (1916-1993):

Swami Chinmayananda provided extensive commentaries on the Panchadasi. He emphasized its practical applicability in modern life, particularly the concept of witnessing consciousness as a means to inner peace.

"The Panchadasi serves as a practical guide for the seeker, systematically unraveling the layers of ignorance to reveal our true nature as non-dual consciousness." - Swami Chinmayananda

2. Sri Ramana Maharshi (1879-1950):

While Ramana Maharshi didn't directly comment on the Panchadasi, his teachings on self-inquiry align closely with its core principles. He emphasized direct experience over intellectual understanding.

"The essence of Vedanta, as expounded in texts like the Panchadasi, is to turn within and inquire 'Who am I?'" - attributed to Sri Ramana Maharshi

3. Swami Dayananda Saraswati (1930-2015):

Swami Dayananda provided in-depth analyses of the Panchadasi, particularly emphasizing its logical structure and its role in resolving the seeming contradiction between individual experience and non-dual reality.

"The Panchadasi beautifully unfolds the vision of Advaita, addressing common objections and misconceptions with remarkable clarity." - Swami Dayananda Saraswati

4. Sri Nisargadatta Maharaj (1897-1981):

While not directly commenting on the Panchadasi, Nisargadatta's teachings on consciousness and identity closely parallel its core concepts.

"What the Panchadasi describes intellectually, one must realize experientially. The 'I am' consciousness is your true nature." - paraphrased from Sri Nisargadatta Maharaj's teachings

5. Dr. Robert Svoboda (1953-present):

A modern Ayurvedic practitioner and scholar, Dr. Svoboda has drawn parallels between the Panchadasi's model of consciousness and modern psychological theories.

"The Panchadasi's description of the five sheaths offers a sophisticated model of human psychology that is still relevant today." - Dr. Robert Svoboda

Contemporary Relevance:

The Panchadasi continues to be studied and applied in various contexts:

1. **Psychology:** Its model of consciousness and identity is being explored in transpersonal psychology.

2. **Mindfulness:** The concept of sakshi (witness consciousness) aligns with modern mindfulness practices.

3. **Cognitive Science:** The text's analysis of perception and cognition is being compared with contemporary theories of mind.

4. **Ethics:** Its non-dual perspective offers a foundation for environmental and social ethics.

This overview provides a foundation for understanding the Panchadasi and its contemporary relevance. For a deeper exploration, consulting the original text and the works of the mentioned scholars and spiritual teachers is recommended.

Resources:

Swami Sarvapriyananda on Panchadasi - Playlist of 13 videos

https://youtube.com/playlist?list=

PLAjdUvxpOY7VnvEMvjWvcYyaDmxmKGIBk&si

=NdAsP3h5XxjlOEx8

Appendix B The Brihadaranyaka Upanishad

Hari Om

The Brihadaranyaka Upanishad: Ancient Wisdom for Modern Life

1. Introduction

The Brihadaranyaka Upanishad is one of the oldest and most significant of the ancient Indian philosophical texts known as the Upanishads. Its name can be translated as "The Great Forest Text" or "The Great Book of the Secret Doctrine of the Forest." Composed around 700-600 BCE, it is a cornerstone of Vedantic philosophy and has profoundly influenced Hindu thought and spirituality for millennia.

This Upanishad is renowned for its depth, breadth, and philosophical richness. It explores fundamental questions about the nature of reality, consciousness, the self (Atman), and the ultimate reality (Brahman). The text is structured as a series of dialogues and teachings, often using metaphors and allegories to convey complex spiritual concepts.

In this extensive exploration, we will delve into the key teachings of the Brihadaranyaka Upanishad, examine its structure and content, and consider how its ancient wisdom can be applied to modern life. We will also incorporate insights from contemporary scholars and spiritual leaders who continue to find relevance and inspiration in this timeless text.

2. Structure and Content Overview

The Brihadaranyaka Upanishad is divided into three Kandas (sections), each containing two Adhyayas (chapters), for a total of six chapters. These are:

1. Madhu Kanda (The Book of Honey)
2. Yajnavalkya Kanda (The Book of Yajnavalkya)
3. Khila Kanda (The Supplementary Book)

Each section contains various philosophical discussions, rituals, and teachings. The text is primarily associated with the Shukla

Yajurveda and is part of the Shatapatha Brahmana.

3. Key Themes and Concepts

3.1 The Nature of Reality

One of the central themes of the Brihadaranyaka Upanishad is the nature of ultimate reality. It posits that behind the apparent diversity of the universe lies a single, unified consciousness known as Brahman. This concept is famously expressed in the mahavakya (great saying): "Aham Brahmasmi" (I am Brahman).

Contemporary relevance: In our increasingly interconnected world, this ancient idea of underlying unity resonates with modern scientific understandings of the interconnectedness of all things. It can inspire a sense of global consciousness and environmental responsibility.

3.2 The Self (Atman)

The Upanishad teaches that the individual self (Atman) is ultimately identical with Brahman. This realization is considered the highest spiritual knowledge.

Contemporary relevance: This concept can be seen as promoting self-understanding and self-realization. In a world often focused on external achievements, the Upanishad's emphasis on inner knowledge offers a counterbalance, encouraging introspection and personal growth.

3.3 The Nature of Knowledge

The text explores different types of knowledge, emphasizing the distinction between intellectual understanding and experiential realization.

Contemporary relevance: In our information-rich age, this distinction is particularly pertinent. It reminds us of the value of direct experience and intuitive understanding alongside intellectual knowledge.

4. The Madhu Kanda (Book of Honey)

The first section of the Upanishad is called the Madhu Kanda or the "Book of Honey." This name comes from its teaching that just as honey is the essence of flowers, the divine Self (Atman) is the essence of all existence.

4.1 The Cosmic Horse Sacrifice

The Upanishad begins with a description of the Ashvamedha (horse sacrifice) ritual, using it as a metaphor for the cosmos. Each part of the horse is equated with different aspects of the universe, illustrating the interconnectedness of all things.

Contemporary relevance: While the literal horse sacrifice is no longer practiced, the metaphor can be understood as emphasizing the sacredness and interconnectedness of all aspects of life. It encourages us to see the divine in the ordinary and to treat all of existence with reverence.

4.2 The Primordial Self

The text then describes the creation of the world from the primordial Self. It states that in the beginning, there was only the Self in the form of a person (Purusha). This Self then divided itself into male and female, which then took on various forms, creating all beings.

Contemporary relevance: This creation myth can be seen as a metaphor for the fundamental unity underlying all diversity. It can inspire a perspective that sees all beings as manifestations of the same underlying reality, promoting empathy and compassion.

4.3 The Five Sheaths

The Upanishad describes five sheaths (koshas) that cover the Self:

1. Annamaya kosha (food sheath)
2. Pranamaya kosha (vital air sheath)
3. Manomaya kosha (mind sheath)
4. Vijnanamaya kosha (intellect sheath)
5. Anandamaya kosha (bliss sheath)

Contemporary relevance: This concept offers a holistic model of human existence, encompassing physical, energetic, mental, intellectual, and spiritual dimensions. It can be used as a framework for comprehensive well-being practices, addressing all aspects of human life.

5. The Yajnavalkya Kanda (Book of Yajnavalkya)

This section primarily features the teachings of the sage Yajnavalkya, considered one of the greatest philosophers in the Upanishadic tradition.

5.1 Dialogue with Maitreyi

One of the most famous passages in this section is Yajnavalkya's dialogue with his wife Maitreyi. When Yajnavalkya decides to renounce the world, Maitreyi asks him if wealth can bring her immortality. Yajnavalkya replies that wealth can provide comfort but not immortality or ultimate fulfilment. He then proceeds to teach her about the nature of the Self and true immortality.

Contemporary relevance: This dialogue offers a profound critique of materialism, highly relevant in our consumer-driven society. It encourages us to look beyond material wealth for true fulfilment and to prioritize spiritual growth and self-knowledge.

5.2 The Nature of Brahman

Yajnavalkya provides various descriptions of Brahman, often using the famous "neti, neti" (not this, not this) approach. This method of negation is used to point to the ineffable nature of ultimate reality.

Contemporary relevance: The "neti, neti" approach can be seen as a form of critical thinking, encouraging us to question our assumptions and go beyond surface appearances. It promotes a mindset of continuous inquiry and openness to the unknown.

6. Applying the Wisdom of the Brihadaranyaka Upanishad in Daily Life

While the Brihadaranyaka Upanishad deals with profound philosophical concepts, its teachings can be practically applied to enhance our daily lives:

6.1 Cultivating Self-Awareness

The Upanishad's emphasis on self-knowledge can inspire us to engage in regular self-reflection and mindfulness practices. This can lead to greater emotional intelligence, better decision-making, and improved relationships.

6.2 Recognizing Unity in Diversity

The teaching of the underlying unity of all existence can foster a more inclusive and compassionate worldview. It can help us overcome prejudices and see the common humanity in all people.

6.3 Balancing Material and Spiritual Pursuits

The dialogue between Yajnavalkya and Maitreyi reminds us to balance our material pursuits with spiritual growth. This can lead to a more fulfilling and purposeful life.

6.4 Embracing Impermanence

The Upanishad's teachings on the transient nature of worldly things can help us develop detachment and resilience in the face of life's ups and downs.

6.5 Practicing Holistic Well-being

The concept of the five sheaths (koshas) can guide us in adopting a holistic approach to health and well-being, addressing physical, energetic, mental, intellectual, and spiritual aspects of our lives.

7. The Khila Kanda (The Supplementary Book)

The Khila Kanda, or the Supplementary Book, is the third and final section of the Brihadaranyaka Upanishad. This section contains various teachings and rituals, some of which are more esoteric in nature. It also includes further philosophical discussions that build upon the concepts introduced in the earlier sections.

7.1 The Prajapati's Instructions

One of the notable passages in this section involves the instructions of Prajapati (the creator) to the three classes of beings: gods, humans, and demons. To each, Prajapati utters the syllable "Da" and asks them to understand its meaning.

- To the gods, who are naturally inclined towards pleasure, "Da" means "Damyata" (self-control).

- To humans, who are naturally inclined towards greed, "Da" means "Datta" (give).

- To the demons, who are naturally inclined towards cruelty, "Da" means "Dayadhvam" (compassion).

Contemporary relevance: This teaching can be seen as a guide for balanced living. It suggests that different aspects of our personality need different virtues to achieve harmony. In our daily lives, we can practice self-control in our indulgences, generosity in our dealings with others, and compassion in our judgments.

7.2 The Five Fires Doctrine

The Khila Kanda also contains the doctrine of the five fires (Panchagni Vidya), which describes the cycle of birth and rebirth. It metaphorically equates various cosmic and natural processes to sacrificial fires.

Contemporary relevance: While the literal interpretation may not resonate with modern scientific understanding, the underlying principle of interconnectedness between cosmic processes and individual life can inspire a more holistic and ecological worldview. It can encourage us to see our lives as part of larger natural cycles and to live in harmony with nature.

7.3 The Concept of Karma and Rebirth

The Upanishad elaborates on the concepts of karma and rebirth, explaining how one's actions in this life determine future experiences.

Contemporary relevance: The concept of karma can be understood as a principle of cause and effect in the moral realm. It encourages personal responsibility and ethical living. Even if one doesn't believe in literal rebirth, the idea that our actions have far-reaching consequences can motivate us to act with greater consideration and mindfulness.

8. Key Philosophical Concepts and Their Modern Applications

8.1 Non-Dualism (Advaita)

The Brihadaranyaka Upanishad is a cornerstone text for the philosophy of Advaita Vedanta, which posits the non-dual nature of reality. It teaches that the individual self (Atman) and the ultimate reality (Brahman) are one and the same.

Contemporary relevance: This non-dual perspective can be applied to overcome divisions and promote unity. In a world often divided by ideologies, religions, and nationalities, the recognition of underlying oneness can foster peace and cooperation. On a personal level, it can help overcome feelings of isolation and disconnection.

8.2 The Nature of Consciousness

The Upanishad delves deep into the nature of consciousness, describing it as the ultimate reality underlying all existence.

Contemporary relevance: This ancient exploration of consciousness resonates with modern scientific investigations into the nature of mind and awareness. It can inspire a more expansive view of consciousness, encouraging us to explore our own awareness through practices like meditation and mindfulness.

8.3 The Concept of Maya

While not explicitly named as such in the Brihadaranyaka Upanishad, the concept of Maya (illusion) is implicit in its teachings about the nature of reality.

Contemporary relevance: The idea of Maya can be understood as a reminder to question our perceptions and assumptions. In an era of information overload and "fake news," this ancient concept encourages critical thinking and discernment.

9. Contemporary Interpretations and Commentaries

Many modern scholars and spiritual leaders have found continued relevance in the teachings of the Brihadaranyaka Upanishad. Here are some contemporary perspectives:

9.1 Swami Vivekananda's Interpretation

Swami Vivekananda, the 19th-century Indian monk who introduced Vedanta philosophy to the Western world, drew heavily from the Brihadaranyaka Upanishad. He emphasized its teachings on the divinity of the soul and the unity of existence as a basis for social reform and universal brotherhood.

9.2 Ken Wilber's Integral Theory

Contemporary philosopher Ken Wilber has incorporated Upanishadic concepts, including those from the Brihadaranyaka Upanishad, into his Integral Theory. He sees the Upanishadic teaching of non-dual awareness as representing the highest stage of consciousness development.

9.3 Quantum Physics and Non-Duality

Some modern physicists, such as Fritjof Capra in "The Tao of Physics," have drawn parallels between the non-dual philosophy of the Upanishads and the implications of quantum physics. While these comparisons are not without controversy, they highlight the continued relevance of ancient Indian philosophy in modern scientific discourse.

10. Practices Inspired by the Brihadaranyaka Upanishad

The teachings of this Upanishad have inspired various spiritual and philosophical practices. Here are some ways to incorporate its wisdom into daily life:

10.1 Self-Inquiry (Atma Vichara)

Inspired by the Upanishad's emphasis on self-knowledge, the practice of self-inquiry involves continually questioning "Who am I?" to pierce through layers of false identification and realize one's true nature.

10.2 Meditation on "I Am" (Aham Brahmasmi)

This meditation involves focusing on the sense of "I am," inspired by the Upanishadic mahavakya "Aham Brahmasmi" (I am Brahman). It's a practice aimed at realizing one's identity with the ultimate reality.

10.3 Witness Consciousness Practice

Based on the Upanishad's teachings about the nature of consciousness, this practice involves cultivating awareness of one's thoughts and experiences without identifying with them.

10.4 Karma Yoga

While not explicitly outlined in the Brihadaranyaka Upanishad, the concept of Karma Yoga (selfless action) is derived from its teachings on the nature of action and its consequences. This involves performing one's duties without attachment to the results.

11. Challenges in Interpreting and Applying the Brihadaranyaka Upanishad

While the Brihadaranyaka Upanishad contains profound wisdom, it also presents certain challenges for modern readers and practitioners:

11.1 Cultural and Historical Context

The text was composed in a specific cultural and historical context, which can make some of its references and rituals difficult for modern readers to understand or relate to.

11.2 Symbolic and Esoteric Language

The Upanishad often uses highly symbolic and esoteric language, which can be challenging to interpret without guidance from a knowledgeable teacher.

11.3 Philosophical Complexity

The philosophical concepts discussed in the Upanishad are often subtle and complex, requiring deep study and contemplation to grasp fully.

11.4 Potential for Misinterpretation

The non-dual philosophy of the Upanishad can sometimes be misinterpreted as a justification for ethical relativism or a denial of the practical realities of daily life.

12. The Brihadaranyaka Upanishad in the Context of World Philosophy

The Brihadaranyaka Upanishad's influence extends beyond Indian philosophy. Its ideas have parallels and resonances with various philosophical and spiritual traditions worldwide:

12.1 Similarities with Neoplatonism

The Upanishad's concept of an ultimate, unifying reality (Brahman) bears similarities to the Neoplatonic concept of "The One."

12.2 Parallels with Mystical Traditions

The experiential, non-dual realization described in the Upanishad has parallels in mystical traditions across religions, including Sufism in Islam and contemplative Christianity.

12.3 Influence on Modern Philosophy

Philosophers like Arthur Schopenhauer and Ralph Waldo Emerson were deeply influenced by Upanishadic thought, including ideas from the Brihadaranyaka Upanishad.

13. Conclusion: The Enduring Relevance of the Brihadaranyaka Upanishad

The Brihadaranyaka Upanishad, despite its ancient origins, continues to offer profound insights relevant to modern life. Its teachings on the nature of reality, consciousness, and the self provide a framework for understanding our place in the universe and our relationship with others and the world around us.

In our fast-paced, often materialistic modern world, the Upanishad's emphasis on self-knowledge, ethical living, and the quest for ultimate truth offers a valuable counterbalance. It reminds us to look beyond surface appearances, to question our assumptions, and to seek a deeper understanding of ourselves and the world.

The text's non-dual philosophy, while challenging to fully grasp, offers a vision of unity that could contribute to solving many of the world's problems rooted in division and conflict. Its teachings on the interconnectedness of all things resonate with modern ecological awareness and can inspire a more sustainable way of living.

Moreover, the practices inspired by the Upanishad, such as self-inquiry and meditation, offer practical tools for personal growth and self-realization. These practices can help us navigate the complexities of modern life with greater awareness, compassion, and equanimity.

As we continue to grapple with fundamental questions about the nature of existence, consciousness, and meaning, the Brihadaranyaka Upanishad remains a rich source of wisdom and inspiration. Its enduring relevance is a testament to the universal and timeless nature of its insights into the human condition and the nature of reality.

In conclusion, while the Brihadaranyaka Upanishad emerged from a specific cultural and historical context, its core teachings transcend time and culture. By engaging with this text - studying it, reflecting on its teachings, and applying its wisdom to our lives - we can tap into a profound source of knowledge that has the potential to transform our understanding of ourselves and the world around us.

Expert Comments on the Brihadaranyaka Upanishad:

1. Dr. Anantanand Rambachan, Professor of Religion at St. Olaf College:

Dr. Rambachan emphasizes the Upanishad's teaching on the nature of the self: "The Brihadaranyaka Upanishad presents one of the most profound and comprehensive expositions of the nature of the self (atman) in the Upanishadic tradition. It argues for the identity of the individual self with the universal self and offers a vision of human fulfilment through this knowledge."

2. Dr. Robert Thurman, Professor of Indo-Tibetan Buddhist Studies at Columbia University:

Dr. Thurman highlights the text's philosophical depth: "The Brihadaranyaka Upanishad is a cornerstone of Indian philosophy. Its explorations of consciousness, reality, and the self are not merely abstract philosophies but are intended as practical guides for the transformation of human experience."

3. Dr. Jonardon Ganeri, Professor of Philosophy at NYU:

Dr. Ganeri notes the Upanishad's epistemological contributions: "The Brihadaranyaka Upanishad offers sophisticated reflections on the nature of knowledge and consciousness. Its discussions on these topics anticipate many debates in contemporary philosophy of mind and epistemology."

4. Swami Vivekananda:

Although not a contemporary expert, Swami Vivekananda's interpretation remains influential. He said: "The Brihadaranyaka Upanishad is one of the greatest works on philosophy and religion ever written anywhere. It is the most authoritative and most ancient of the Upanishads."

5. Dr. Deepak Chopra, author and alternative medicine advocate:

Dr. Chopra often refers to the Brihadaranyaka Upanishad in his work: "This ancient text provides a roadmap for self-realization and understanding the nature of consciousness. Its teachings on non-duality offer a perspective that can revolutionize our understanding of reality and our place in it."

Applying the Teachings of the Brihadaranyaka Upanishad in Daily Life:

1. Self-Reflection and Self-Inquiry:

The Upanishad emphasizes the importance of self-knowledge. We can incorporate this by:

- Setting aside time each day for introspection and self-reflection.

- Practicing mindfulness to become more aware of our thoughts, emotions, and reactions.

- Regularly asking ourselves profound questions like "Who am I?" to deepen our self-understanding.

2. Cultivating Non-Attachment:

The text teaches about the transient nature of worldly things. We can apply this by:

- Practicing gratitude for what we have while not clinging to possessions or outcomes.

- Developing resilience in the face of change and loss.

- Focusing on inner growth rather than external achievements.

3. Recognizing Unity in Diversity:

The Upanishad's non-dual philosophy can be applied in daily life by:

- Cultivating empathy and compassion for others, recognizing our shared humanity.

- Actively working to overcome prejudices and biases.

- Engaging in activities that promote social harmony and mutual understanding.

4. Ethical Living:

The concept of karma in the Upanishad encourages ethical behavior. We can:

- Make conscious choices, considering the long-term consequences of our actions.

- Practice honesty and integrity in all our dealings.

- Engage in acts of kindness and service to others.

5. Balancing Material and Spiritual Pursuits:

Drawing from the dialogue between Yajnavalkya and Maitreyi, we can:

- Reassess our priorities, ensuring we're not solely focused on material gain.

- Allocate time and resources for spiritual growth and self-development.

- Find ways to infuse our work and daily activities with a sense of higher purpose.

6. Cultivating Witness Consciousness:

Based on the Upanishad's teachings on consciousness, we can:

- Practice observing our thoughts and emotions without immediately reacting to them.

- Develop a more objective perspective on our experiences.

- Use meditation techniques that cultivate a sense of detached awareness.

7. Embracing Interconnectedness:

The Upanishad's vision of cosmic unity can inspire us to:

- Make environmentally conscious choices, recognizing our connection to nature.

- Cultivate relationships based on mutual respect and understanding.

- Engage in practices that promote a sense of connection with all of life.

8. Continuous Learning and Questioning:

The "neti, neti" (not this, not this) approach can be applied by:

- Cultivating intellectual humility and openness to new ideas.

- Regularly challenging our assumptions and beliefs.

- Engaging in lifelong learning and intellectual exploration.

9. Practicing Holistic Well-being:

Drawing from the concept of the five sheaths (koshas), we can:

- Adopt a comprehensive approach to health, addressing physical, energetic, mental, intellectual, and spiritual aspects.

- Engage in practices that nurture each of these dimensions, such as yoga, pranayama, meditation, study, and service.

10. Finding the Sacred in the Ordinary:

Inspired by the Upanishad's vision of the divine permeating all existence, we can:

- Cultivate a sense of wonder and appreciation for everyday experiences.

- Perform our daily tasks with mindfulness and reverence.

- Recognize the potential for spiritual growth in all aspects of life.

By integrating these practices into our daily lives, we can bring the profound wisdom of the Brihadaranyaka Upanishad into practical application, potentially leading to greater self-awareness, ethical living, and a deeper sense of connection with ourselves, others, and the world around us.

Resources:

Swami Anubhavananda Saraswati - play list of 49 videos on Brihadaranyaka Upanishad

https://youtube.com/playlist?list=
PLAF_c2xr3i8Dg8P9I5hMyJftyvGtzE9WS&si
=Mb4uQVHyf0M6LCRA

Appendix C Chandogya Upanishad

Hari Om

The Chandogya Upanishad is one of the oldest and most important Upanishads in Hindu philosophy. Here's a detailed description:

Contents of the Chandogya Upanishad:

1. Structure: It consists of eight chapters (prapathakas) divided into numerous sections.

2. Origin: It's part of the Sama Veda and is associated with the Chandoga school of Vedic chanting.

3. Key themes:

- The nature of Brahman (ultimate reality)

- The concept of Atman (individual soul) and its relation to Brahman

- The significance of Om (sacred syllable)

- The importance of meditation and self-knowledge

- Ethical and moral teachings

4. Notable teachings:

- "Tat Tvam Asi" (That Thou Art) - one of the Mahavakyas of Vedanta

- The concept of space (akasha) as a metaphor for Brahman

- The importance of food and breath in sustaining life

- The nature of mind and consciousness

- The concept of rebirth and karma

5. Philosophical discussions:

- Dialogues between teachers and students

- Allegorical stories to illustrate spiritual concepts

- Explanations of rituals and their deeper meanings

Relevance in modern daily life:

1. Self-realization: The Upanishad's emphasis on self-knowledge can help individuals understand their true nature and potential.

2. Mindfulness: Its teachings on meditation can be applied to modern mindfulness practices for stress reduction and mental clarity.

3. Ethical living: The moral teachings provide guidance for leading a virtuous life in today's complex world.

4. Interconnectedness: The concept of unity between individual and universal consciousness can foster a sense of global community.

5. Environmental awareness: The Upanishad's reverence for nature can inspire eco-friendly attitudes and practices.

6. Holistic health: Its teachings on the importance of breath and food align with modern holistic approaches to health and well-being.

7. Problem-solving: The analytical and questioning approach demonstrated in the text can be applied to critical thinking in various aspects of life.

8. Dealing with change: The philosophical insights can help individuals cope with life's uncertainties and changes.

Comments from contemporary exponents of spirituality:

1. Sri Sri Ravi Shankar: He has emphasized the Chandogya Upanishad's teachings on the power of intention and the importance of living in the present moment.

2. Swami Vivekananda: Although not contemporary, his interpretations continue to influence modern thought. He highlighted the Upanishad's message of strength and self-reliance.

3. Deepak Chopra: He has drawn parallels between the Upanishad's teachings and modern quantum physics, particularly regarding consciousness and reality.

4. Sadhguru Jaggi Vasudev: He has spoken about the Upanishad's relevance to understanding the nature of existence and the path to self-realization.

5. Radhanath Swami: He has emphasized the Upanishad's teachings on the importance of guru-disciple relationship in spiritual growth.

Part 1: Introduction and Historical Context

The Chandogya Upanishad is one of the principal Upanishads of Hinduism, forming part of the Sama Veda. It is considered one of the oldest and most important Upanishads, dating back to the Vedic period, approximately 800-600 BCE. The name "Chandogya" is derived from the word "Chandoga," which refers to the priests who chant the Sama Veda.

Historical Context:

The Upanishads emerged during a time of significant philosophical and spiritual inquiry in ancient India. This period, often referred to as the Axial Age, saw the development of new ideas and philosophies across various civilizations. In India, this manifested as a shift from the earlier Vedic emphasis on external rituals to a more introspective and philosophical approach to understanding reality and the self.

The Chandogya Upanishad, like other major Upanishads, represents this shift. It retains elements of Vedic ritual and symbolism but reinterprets them in light of deeper philosophical and spiritual insights.

Structure and Composition:

The Chandogya Upanishad consists of eight chapters (prapathakas), each divided into numerous sections (khandas). The text is primarily in prose, interspersed with some verses. It employs various teaching methods, including dialogues, stories, analogies, and direct instructions.

Part 2: Key Themes and Concepts

1. Brahman and Atman:

The central theme of the Chandogya Upanishad, as with most Upanishads, is the nature of Brahman (the ultimate reality) and its relationship to Atman (the individual self). The text explores various aspects of Brahman, often through analogies and stories, and ultimately asserts the fundamental unity of Brahman and Atman.

2. The Significance of Om:

The Upanishad emphasizes the importance of the sacred syllable Om, describing it as the essence of all things and a means to realize Brahman. It equates Om with Udgitha, the principal part of Sama Veda chants, thus linking Vedic ritual with philosophical understanding.

3. The Nature of Reality:

Through various teachings and stories, the Upanishad delves into the nature of reality, consciousness, and existence. It often uses elements of the physical world (such as space, air, fire) as metaphors for deeper spiritual truths.

4. Ethics and Moral Teachings:

While primarily focused on metaphysical concepts, the Chandogya Upanishad also imparts ethical and moral teachings, emphasizing virtues such as truthfulness, self-control, and compassion.

5. The Importance of Knowledge and Self-Realization:

A recurring theme is the paramount importance of knowledge, particularly self-knowledge, in achieving liberation (moksha) from the cycle of birth and death.

Part 3: Notable Teachings and Stories

1. Tat Tvam Asi (That Thou Art):

One of the most famous teachings from the Chandogya Upanishad is the mahavakya (great saying) "Tat Tvam Asi," which appears in the sixth chapter. This profound statement asserts the unity of the individual self (Atman) with the ultimate reality (Brahman).

In this section, the sage Uddalaka Aruni instructs his son Svetaketu about the nature of reality. Through a series of examples and analogies, he leads Svetaketu to understand that the essence of all things is the same, and that this essence is identical with the self. The phrase "Tat Tvam Asi" is repeated nine times, emphasizing its importance.

2. The Story of Satyakama Jabala:

This story, found in the fourth chapter, illustrates the importance of truthfulness and the idea that spiritual knowledge is not confined to any particular social class. Satyakama, not knowing his father's identity, honestly admits this when seeking a teacher.

His truthfulness is seen as a sign of his worthiness to receive spiritual instruction.

3. The Allegory of Salt and Water:

In another teaching to Svetaketu, Uddalaka uses the analogy of salt dissolved in water to illustrate the omnipresence and subtlety of Brahman. Just as salt, when dissolved, cannot be seen but is tasted throughout the water, so too is Brahman imperceptible yet present in all things.

4. The Concept of Prana (Vital Breath):

The Upanishad contains several discussions on the nature and importance of prana, often describing it as the essence of life and consciousness. These teachings have had a significant influence on later Yogic and Tantric practices.

5. The Five Fires Doctrine:

This doctrine, presented in the fifth chapter, describes the cycle of rebirth using the metaphor of five fires. It provides an early exposition of the concepts of karma and reincarnation.

Part 4: Philosophical and Metaphysical Concepts

1. The Nature of Brahman:

The Chandogya Upanishad presents various descriptions and analogies to convey the nature of Brahman. It is described as the source of all existence, beyond all qualities yet manifesting as all qualities, infinitely small yet infinitely vast. The text often uses paradoxical statements to point to the transcendent nature of Brahman.

2. Consciousness and Reality:

The Upanishad explores the relationship between consciousness, perception, and reality. It suggests that consciousness is not merely a product of material processes but is fundamental to the nature of reality itself.

3. The Concept of Maya:

While not explicitly using the term "maya," the Chandogya Upanishad lays the groundwork for this important concept in later Vedantic philosophy. It suggests that the apparent multiplicity of the world is ultimately an appearance, behind which lies the unitary reality of Brahman.

4. The States of Consciousness:

The Upanishad discusses different states of consciousness, including waking, dreaming, and deep sleep, as well as a fourth state (turiya) that transcends these. This analysis of consciousness has been highly influential in later Hindu and Buddhist philosophy.

5. The Nature of the Self:

Throughout the text, there are various teachings on the nature of the self (Atman). It is described as immortal, beyond suffering, and identical with Brahman. The Upanishad encourages deep inquiry into the nature of the self as a means to liberation.

Part 5: Relevance to Modern Daily Life

1. Self-Reflection and Personal Growth:

The Upanishad's emphasis on self-knowledge can be applied to modern practices of self-reflection and personal development. Its teachings encourage individuals to look beyond surface-level identities and discover their deeper nature.

2. Mindfulness and Meditation:

The text's discussions on consciousness and the nature of mind align with contemporary mindfulness practices. Its teachings on meditation can be adapted to modern stress-reduction techniques and methods for enhancing mental clarity.

3. Ethical Living:

The moral teachings of the Upanishad, emphasizing truthfulness, compassion, and self-control, provide a framework for ethical decision-making in today's complex world.

4. Holistic Approach to Health:

The Upanishad's understanding of the interconnectedness of mind, body, and spirit resonates with modern holistic health approaches. Its teachings on prana (vital breath) can be related to the importance of proper breathing in physical and mental health.

5. Environmental Consciousness:

The text's portrayal of the natural world as a manifestation of the divine can inspire a more respectful and sustainable approach to the environment.

6. Dealing with Change and Uncertainty:

The philosophical insights of the Upanishad can provide a perspective for coping with life's uncertainties and changes, encouraging a broader view of existence beyond immediate circumstances.

7. Interpersonal Relationships:

The concept of the underlying unity of all beings can foster greater empathy and understanding in personal and professional relationships.

8. Critical Thinking:

The questioning and analytical approach demonstrated in the Upanishad's dialogues can be applied to critical thinking in various aspects of modern life, from education to problem-solving in the workplace.

Part 6: Modern Interpretations and Commentaries

1. Swami Vivekananda:

Although not strictly contemporary, Swami Vivekananda's interpretations continue to influence modern understanding of the Upanishads. He emphasized the Chandogya Upanishad's message of strength and self-reliance, interpreting its teachings in a way that encouraged social reform and national awakening in India.

Vivekananda saw in the Upanishad a call for realizing one's innate divinity and applying this realization to serve humanity. He particularly emphasized the "Tat Tvam Asi" doctrine as a basis for social equality and compassion.

2. Sri Aurobindo:

Sri Aurobindo's interpretation of the Chandogya Upanishad is notable for its integration of spiritual and evolutionary perspectives. He saw in the Upanishad's teachings a blueprint for the evolution of consciousness, both individual and collective.

Aurobindo interpreted the various analogies and stories in the Upanishad as describing different levels of consciousness and the process of their integration. He related the Upanishad's concept of Brahman to his own philosophy of the Supramental consciousness.

3. Ramana Maharshi:

Ramana Maharshi's teachings, while not directly commenting on the Chandogya Upanishad, resonated deeply with its core message. His method of self-inquiry, asking "Who am I?", can be seen as a practical application of the Upanishad's emphasis on self-knowledge.

Maharshi's understanding of the self as pure consciousness aligns closely with the Upanishad's descriptions of Atman and Brahman.

4. Sri Sri Ravi Shankar:

Sri Sri Ravi Shankar has emphasized the practical applications of the Chandogya Upanishad's teachings in modern life. He has spoken about the power of intention and the importance of living in the present moment, drawing from the Upanishad's insights.

He has also interpreted the Upanishad's teachings on prana in relation to modern breath-work and meditation techniques, making these ancient concepts accessible to a contemporary audience.

5. Swami Chinmayananda:

Swami Chinmayananda's commentaries on the Chandogya Upanishad are known for their clarity and modern relevance. He interpreted the text in a way that bridged traditional understanding with contemporary scientific and psychological insights.

His explanations of concepts like consciousness and the nature of reality often drew parallels with modern physics, making the ancient wisdom more relatable to a scientifically educated audience.

Part 7: Scientific and Psychological Perspectives

1. Quantum Physics and Consciousness:

Some modern interpreters, including physicists like Fritjof Capra and philosophers like Ken Wilber, have drawn parallels between the Upanishadic view of consciousness and reality and insights from quantum physics. The Chandogya Upanishad's descriptions of the underlying unity of existence and the role of consciousness in shaping reality have been compared to quantum concepts like non-locality and the observer effect.

2. Neuroscience and States of Consciousness:

The Upanishad's discussions on different states of consciousness have attracted interest from neuroscientists studying altered states of consciousness, meditation, and sleep. Research into meditation and mindfulness practices has found neurological correlates that seem to align with some of the experiences described in the text.

3. Psychology and Self-Concept:

Modern psychological theories of self and identity have found resonance with the Upanishad's teachings on the nature of the self. Concepts from transpersonal psychology, in particular, often draw inspiration from Upanishadic ideas about the expansion of identity beyond the individual ego.

4. Cognitive Science and Perception:

The Upanishad's explorations of the relationship between perception, consciousness, and reality have been of interest to cognitive scientists studying the nature of perception and the construction of subjective reality.

Part 8: Contemporary Applications and Practices

1. Mindfulness and Meditation:

Many modern mindfulness and meditation practices draw inspiration from the Chandogya Upanishad's teachings on consciousness and self-awareness. Techniques that focus on observing thoughts and emotions without attachment can be seen as practical applications of the Upanishad's insights into the nature of mind and self.

2. Yoga Philosophy:

The philosophy and practice of yoga, especially in its more contemplative forms, often incorporates ideas from the Chandogya Upanishad. The concept of prana and its importance in spiritual practice has been particularly influential in the development of pranayama (breath control) techniques.

3. Psychotherapy and Counseling:

Some therapists and counselors have incorporated insights from the Upanishad into their practice, particularly in approaches that emphasize self-discovery and the expansion of self-concept.

The idea that true happiness comes from self-realization rather than external circumstances is often used in therapeutic contexts.

4. Education:

The Upanishad's emphasis on the teacher-student relationship and the process of inquiry has influenced alternative educational approaches. Some educators have drawn on its methods to develop more holistic and inquiry-based learning models.

5. Leadership and Management:

Concepts from the Chandogya Upanishad have been applied in leadership and management training, particularly ideas about self-awareness, ethical behavior, and the interconnectedness of all beings. These principles are sometimes used to promote more conscious and compassionate leadership styles.

6. Environmental Ethics:

The Upanishad's vision of the divine permeating all of nature has been invoked in discussions of environmental ethics and sustainability. It has been used to argue for a more reverent and protective attitude towards the natural world.

Part 9: Challenges and Criticisms

1. Interpretation and Translation:

One of the challenges in understanding and applying the Chandogya Upanishad in the modern context is the difficulty of accurate translation and interpretation. The Sanskrit text often uses metaphors and concepts that don't have direct equivalents in modern languages or thought systems.

2. Cultural Context:

Some critics argue that removing the teachings of the Upanishad from their original cultural and historical context risks misinterpreting or oversimplifying them. There's an ongoing debate about how to make these ancient teachings relevant without losing their essence.

3. Scientific Compatibility:

While some have drawn parallels between Upanishadic concepts and modern scientific theories, others caution against oversimplifying these connections. The danger of reading modern scientific concepts into ancient philosophical texts (and vice versa) is a point of contention among scholars.

4. Practical Application:

There's debate about how to practically apply the often abstract and metaphysical teachings of the Upanishad in everyday life. Some argue that without the context of traditional spiritual practices, the full impact of these teachings may be lost.

5. Exclusivity and Accessibility:

Historically, the study of the Upanishads was restricted to certain groups in Indian society. While this is no longer the case, there are ongoing discussions about how to make these teachings truly accessible to all, regardless of background or education.

Part 10: Future Directions and Potential

1. Interdisciplinary Studies:

There's growing interest in interdisciplinary approaches that combine study of the Upanishads with fields like cognitive science, psychology, and physics. This could lead to new insights and applications of Upanishadic wisdom.

2. Global Ethics:

As the world grapples with global challenges, the Upanishad's vision of underlying unity and interconnectedness could contribute to discussions on global ethics and cooperation.

3. Artificial Intelligence and Consciousness:

As AI technology advances, the Upanishad's explorations of consciousness could become relevant to debates about machine consciousness and the nature of intelligence.

4. Mental Health:

There's potential for further integration of Upanishadic concepts into mental health practices, particularly in areas like stress reduction, addiction treatment, and dealing with existential anxiety.

5. Education Reform:

The Upanishad's model of education, emphasizing inquiry, self-discovery, and the integration of knowledge, could influence future educational reforms, particularly in promoting more holistic and contemplative approaches to learning.

Conclusion:

The Chandogya Upanishad, despite its ancient origins, continues to offer profound insights relevant to modern life and thought. Its exploration of consciousness, reality, ethics, and the nature of self provides a rich source of wisdom that can be applied in various contexts, from personal development to scientific inquiry.

As we navigate the complexities of the 21st century, the timeless teachings of this Upanishad offer a perspective that encourages deep reflection, ethical living, and a broader understanding of our place in the universe. While challenges remain in interpreting and applying these ancient teachings, their potential to contribute to our understanding of ourselves and our world remains significant.

The ongoing dialogue between this ancient text and modern thought demonstrates the enduring relevance of the Chandogya Upanishad, suggesting that it will continue to be a source of inspiration and insight for generations to come.

Resource:

Chandogya Upanishad -

THE BHANDARKAR ORIENTAL RESEARCH INSTITUTE
https://youtu.be/1WtlkII6ZPU?si=Vv7EiCv795WpbD55
Series of 13 videos playlist on Essence of Upanishads-
THE BHANDARKAR ORIENTAL RESEARCH INSTITUTE
https://youtu.be/HmTYhLnVdQ8?si=EUrYHrJ1A4-dA2Pu

Bibliography

Chapter 1: Setting the context

Hinduism:
    1. The Upanishads (various translations)
2. Bhagavad Gita (various translations)
3. Garuda Purana
4. Dasgupta, S. (1922). A History of Indian Philosophy
5. Olivelle, P. (1996). Upanisads (Oxford World's Classics)
6. Flood, G. (1996). An Introduction to Hinduism
    Buddhism:
    7. Bardo Thodol (Tibetan Book of the Dead)
8. Sogyal Rinpoche. (2002). The Tibetan Book of Living and Dying
9. Thurman, R.A.F. (1994). The Tibetan Book of the Dead
10. Lama Zopa Rinpoche. (2015). How to Enjoy Death
11. Gethin, R. (1998). The Foundations of Buddhism
    Christianity:
    12. The Bible (various translations)
13. Augustine of Hippo. City of God
14. Aquinas, T. Summa Theologica
15. Kübler-Ross, E. (1969). On Death and Dying
16. Lewis, C.S. (1961). A Grief Observed
17. Bowker, J. (1991). The Meanings of Death
    Islam:
    18. The Quran (various translations)
19. Smith, J.I. & Haddad, Y.Y. (2002). The Islamic Understanding of Death and Resurrection
20. Al-Ghazali. (1989). The Remembrance of Death and the Afterlife
21. Chittick, W.C. (1992). Your Sight Today is Piercing: The Muslim Understanding of Death and Afterlife
    Sikhism:

22. Guru Granth Sahib (various translations)

23. Singh, N.K. (2004). Sikhism: An Introduction

24. Cole, W.O. & Sambhi, P.S. (1995). The Sikhs: Their Religious Beliefs and Practices

Indian Philosophy:

25. Radhakrishnan, S. (1923). Indian Philosophy

26. Hiriyanna, M. (1932). Outlines of Indian Philosophy

27. Potter, K.H. (ed.) (1977). Encyclopedia of Indian Philosophies

28. Chatterjee, S. & Datta, D. (1984). An Introduction to Indian Philosophy

Western Philosophy:

29. Plato. Phaedo

30. Epicurus. Letter to Menoeceus

31. Heidegger, M. (1962). Being and Time

32. Sartre, J.P. (1956). Being and Nothingness

33. Schopenhauer, A. (1844). The World as Will and Representation

34. Camus, A. (1955). The Myth of Sisyphus

35. Solomon, R.C. (ed.) (1992). Existentialism

Comparative and Interdisciplinary Studies:

36. Coward, H. (ed.) (1997). Life After Death in World Religions

37. Obayashi, H. (ed.) (1992). Death and Afterlife: Perspectives of World Religions

38. Parkes, C.M., Laungani, P., & Young, B. (eds.) (2015). Death and Bereavement Across Cultures

39. Kastenbaum, R. (2018). Death, Society, and Human Experience

40. Davies, D.J. (2005). A Brief History of Death

Anthropological and Sociological Perspectives:

41. Hertz, R. (1960). Death and the Right Hand

42. Gorer, G. (1965). Death, Grief, and Mourning

43. Aries, P. (1981). The Hour of Our Death

44. Metcalf, P. & Huntington, R. (1991). Celebrations of Death: The Anthropology of Mortuary Ritual

Psychological Perspectives:

45. Becker, E. (1973). The Denial of Death

46. Yalom, I.D. (2008). Staring at the Sun: Overcoming the Terror of Death

47. Kübler-Ross, E. & Kessler, D. (2005). On Grief and Grieving

Chapter 2 : What are key universal thoughts in major religions?

Certainly, I'd be happy to provide a detailed bibliography for this discourse on the universal messages from major world religions. This bibliography includes academic works, primary religious texts, and authoritative sources on comparative religion and individual faith traditions.

Bibliography:

Primary Religious Texts:

1. The Bhagavad Gita (various translations)

2. The Upanishads (various translations)

3. The Tripitaka (Pali Canon)

4. The Hebrew Bible (Tanakh)

5. The Talmud

6. The Christian Bible (various translations)

7. The Quran (various translations)

8. Hadith collections (e.g., Sahih al-Bukhari, Sahih Muslim)

9. Guru Granth Sahib

Comparative Religion:

10. Smith, Huston. (1991). The World's Religions: Our Great Wisdom Traditions. HarperOne.

11. Prothero, Stephen. (2010). God Is Not One: The Eight Rival Religions That Run the World. HarperOne.

12. Smart, Ninian. (1998). The World's Religions. Cambridge University Press.

13. Bowker, John. (1997). World Religions: The Great Faiths Explored and Explained. DK Publishing.

14. Esposito, John L., Fasching, Darrell J., & Lewis, Todd. (2014). World Religions Today. Oxford University Press.

Hinduism:

15. Flood, Gavin. (1996). An Introduction to Hinduism. Cambridge University Press.

16. Klostermaier, Klaus K. (2007). A Survey of Hinduism. SUNY Press.

17. Doniger, Wendy. (2009). The Hindus: An Alternative History. Penguin Press.

Buddhism:

18. Harvey, Peter. (2012). An Introduction to Buddhism: Teachings, History and Practices. Cambridge University Press.

19. Gethin, Rupert. (1998). The Foundations of Buddhism. Oxford University Press.

20. Thich Nhat Hanh. (1999). The Heart of the Buddha's Teaching. Broadway Books.

Judaism:

21. Neusner, Jacob. (2002). Judaism: An Introduction. Penguin Books.

22. Cohn-Sherbok, Dan. (2003). Judaism: History, Belief, and Practice. Routledge.

23. Telushkin, Joseph. (1991). Jewish Literacy. William Morrow & Co.

Christianity:

24. McGrath, Alister E. (2006). Christianity: An Introduction. Blackwell Publishing.

25. Gonzalez, Justo L. (2010). The Story of Christianity (Revised and Updated). HarperOne.

26. MacCulloch, Diarmaid. (2010). Christianity: The First Three Thousand Years. Viking.

Islam:

27. Esposito, John L. (2016). Islam: The Straight Path. Oxford University Press.

28. Armstrong, Karen. (2002). Islam: A Short History. Modern Library.

29. Ramadan, Tariq. (2017). Introduction to Islam. Oxford University Press.

Sikhism:

30. Singh, Nikky-Guninder Kaur. (2011). Sikhism: An Introduction. I.B. Tauris.

31. McLeod, W.H. (1997). Sikhism. Penguin Books.

32. Nesbitt, Eleanor. (2005). Sikhism: A Very Short Introduction. Oxford University Press.

Ethics and Philosophy of Religion:

33. Pojman, Louis P. & Rea, Michael. (2014). Philosophy of Religion: An Anthology. Cengage Learning.

34. Wainwright, William J. (2005). The Oxford Handbook of Philosophy of Religion. Oxford University Press.

35. Quinn, Philip L. & Taliaferro, Charles. (1997). A Companion to Philosophy of Religion. Blackwell Publishing.

Interfaith Dialogue and Religious Pluralism:

36. Knitter, Paul F. (2002). Introducing Theologies of Religions. Orbis Books.

37. Hick, John. (2004). An Interpretation of Religion: Human Responses to the Transcendent. Yale University Press.

38. Swidler, Leonard & Mojzes, Paul. (2000). The Study of Religion in an Age of Global Dialogue. Temple University Press.

Spirituality and Mysticism:

39. Underhill, Evelyn. (2002). Mysticism: A Study in Nature and Development of Spiritual Consciousness. Dover Publications.

40. James, William. (1902). The Varieties of Religious Experience. Longmans, Green & Co.

41. Huxley, Aldous. (2009). The Perennial Philosophy. Harper Perennial Modern Classics.

Chapter 3 : What are key universal thoughts in Oriental and Western Philosophies ?

Eastern Philosophy:

1. Radhakrishnan, S. (1989). Eastern Religions and Western Thought. Oxford University Press.

2. Deutsch, E. (1999). A Companion to World Philosophies. Wiley-Blackwell.

3. Nakamura, H. (1964). Ways of Thinking of Eastern Peoples. University of Hawaii Press.

4. Kalupahana, D.J. (1986). Nagarjuna: The Philosophy of the Middle Way. SUNY Press.

5. Mohanty, J.N. (2000). Classical Indian Philosophy. Rowman & Littlefield Publishers.

6. Ames, R.T. & Rosemont, H. (1998). The Analects of Confucius: A Philosophical Translation. Ballantine Books.

7. Watson, B. (1996). Chuang Tzu: Basic Writings. Columbia University Press.

Western Philosophy:

8. Russell, B. (1945). A History of Western Philosophy. Simon & Schuster.

9. Copleston, F. (1993). A History of Philosophy (9 Volumes). Image.

10. Kenny, A. (2010). A New History of Western Philosophy. Oxford University Press.

11. Scruton, R. (2001). A Short History of Modern Philosophy. Routledge.

12. Blackburn, S. (2008). The Oxford Dictionary of Philosophy. Oxford University Press.

Comparative Philosophy:

13. Scharfstein, B-A. (1998). A Comparative History of World Philosophy: From the Upanishads to Kant. SUNY Press.

14. Raju, P.T. (1962). Introduction to Comparative Philosophy. University of Nebraska Press.

15. Larson, G.J. & Deutsch, E. (1988). Interpreting Across Boundaries: New Essays in Comparative Philosophy. Princeton University Press.

16. Solomon, R.C. & Higgins, K.M. (2003). From Africa to Zen: An Invitation to World Philosophy. Rowman & Littlefield Publishers.

Existential Themes:

17. Sartre, J-P. (1956). Being and Nothingness. Washington Square Press.

18. Heidegger, M. (1962). Being and Time. Harper Perennial Modern Classics.

19. Camus, A. (1955). The Myth of Sisyphus and Other Essays. Vintage.

20. Kierkegaard, S. (1980). The Concept of Anxiety. Princeton University Press.

21. Nishitani, K. (1982). Religion and Nothingness. University of California Press.

22. Tillich, P. (1952). The Courage to Be. Yale University Press.

Consciousness and Self:

23. Dennett, D. (1991). Consciousness Explained. Back Bay Books.

24. Chalmers, D. (1996). The Conscious Mind: In Search of a Fundamental Theory. Oxford University Press.

25. Strawson, G. (2009). Selves: An Essay in Revisionary Metaphysics. Oxford University Press.

26. Zahavi, D. (2005). Subjectivity and Selfhood: Investigating the First-Person Perspective. MIT Press.

27. Siderits, M., Thompson, E., & Zahavi, D. (Eds.) (2010). Self, No Self?: Perspectives from Analytical, Phenomenological, and Indian Traditions. Oxford University Press.

Ethics and Morality:

28. MacIntyre, A. (2007). After Virtue: A Study in Moral Theory. University of Notre Dame Press.

29. Singer, P. (2011). Practical Ethics. Cambridge University Press.

30. Noddings, N. (2013). Caring: A Relational Approach to Ethics and Moral Education. University of California Press.

31. Wong, D.B. (2006). Natural Moralities: A Defense of Pluralistic Relativism. Oxford University Press.

Epistemology and Truth:

32. Williams, M. (2001). Problems of Knowledge: A Critical Introduction to Epistemology. Oxford University Press.

33. Moser, P.K. (2002). The Oxford Handbook of Epistemology. Oxford University Press.

34. Goldman, A.I. (1986). Epistemology and Cognition. Harvard University Press.

35. Sosa, E. (2007). A Virtue Epistemology: Apt Belief and Reflective Knowledge, Volume I. Oxford University Press.

Time and Temporality:

36. McTaggart, J.E. (1908). The Unreality of Time. Mind, 17, 457-474.

37. Husserl, E. (1991). On the Phenomenology of the Consciousness of Internal Time. Springer.

38. Ricoeur, P. (1984-1988). Time and Narrative (3 Volumes). University of Chicago Press.

39. Gödel, K. (1949). An Example of a New Type of Cosmological Solutions of Einstein's Field Equations of Gravitation. Reviews of Modern Physics, 21(3), 447.

Freedom and Determinism:

40. Kane, R. (2005). A Contemporary Introduction to Free Will. Oxford University Press.

41. Dennett, D. (2003). Freedom Evolves. Viking Books.

42. Van Inwagen, P. (1983). An Essay on Free Will. Oxford University Press.

43. Fischer, J.M. (1994). The Metaphysics of Free Will: An Essay on Control. Wiley-Blackwell.

Chapter 4: Importance of subjective experience in quest for ultimate reality

Eastern Philosophical and Religious Perspectives:

1. Deutsch, E. (1969). Advaita Vedanta: A Philosophical Reconstruction. University of Hawaii Press.

2. Radhakrishnan, S. (1953). The Principal Upanishads. Harper.

3. Suzuki, D.T. (1964). An Introduction to Zen Buddhism. Grove Press.

4. Nagarjuna. (1995). The Fundamental Wisdom of the Middle Way. (J. Garfield, Trans.). Oxford University Press.

5. Patanjali. (2015). The Yoga Sutras of Patanjali. (E. Bryant, Trans.). North Point Press.

6. Lao Tzu. (1988). Tao Te Ching. (S. Mitchell, Trans.). Harper Perennial.

7. Bhikkhu Bodhi. (2005). In the Buddha's Words: An Anthology of Discourses from the Pali Canon. Wisdom Publications.

Western Philosophical and Religious Perspectives:

8. Plato. (2000). The Republic. (G.R.F. Ferrari, Ed., T. Griffith, Trans.). Cambridge University Press.

9. Aristotle. (2009). Nicomachean Ethics. (W. D. Ross, Trans.). Oxford University Press.

10. Descartes, R. (1641/1984). Meditations on First Philosophy. In The Philosophical Writings of Descartes. Cambridge University Press.

11. Kant, I. (1781/1998). Critique of Pure Reason. (P. Guyer & A. Wood, Trans.). Cambridge University Press.

12. Kierkegaard, S. (1843/1987). Either/Or. (H.V. Hong & E.H. Hong, Trans.). Princeton University Press.

13. James, W. (1902). The Varieties of Religious Experience. Longmans, Green & Co.

14. Wittgenstein, L. (1953). Philosophical Investigations. (G.E.M. Anscombe, Trans.). Macmillan.

Modern and Contemporary Perspectives:

15. Heidegger, M. (1927/1962). Being and Time. (J. Macquarrie & E. Robinson, Trans.). Harper & Row.

16. Sartre, J.P. (1943/1992). Being and Nothingness. (H.E. Barnes, Trans.). Washington Square Press.

17. Merleau-Ponty, M. (1945/2012). Phenomenology of Perception. (D.A. Landes, Trans.). Routledge.

18. Buber, M. (1923/1970). I and Thou. (W. Kaufmann, Trans.). Charles Scribner's Sons.

19. Maslow, A.H. (1964). Religions, Values, and Peak-Experiences. Ohio State University Press.

20. Wilber, K. (2000). Integral Psychology: Consciousness, Spirit, Psychology, Therapy. Shambhala.

21. Taylor, C. (2007). A Secular Age. Harvard University Press.

Comparative and Integrative Approaches:

22. Smart, N. (1999). World Philosophies. Routledge.

23. Armstrong, K. (1993). A History of God: The 4,000-Year Quest of Judaism, Christianity and Islam. Ballantine Books.

24. Hick, J. (2004). An Interpretation of Religion: Human Responses to the Transcendent. Yale University Press.

25. Smith, H. (1991). The World's Religions. HarperOne.

26. Capra, F. (1975). The Tao of Physics: An Exploration of the Parallels Between Modern Physics and Eastern Mysticism. Shambhala.

Cognitive Science and Psychology of Religion:

27. Newberg, A., D'Aquili, E., & Rause, V. (2001). Why God Won't Go Away: Brain Science and the Biology of Belief. Ballantine Books.

28. Boyer, P. (2001). Religion Explained: The Evolutionary Origins of Religious Thought. Basic Books.

29. Csikszentmihalyi, M. (1990). Flow: The Psychology of Optimal Experience. Harper & Row.

30. Kahneman, D. (2011). Thinking, Fast and Slow. Farrar, Straus and Giroux.

Mysticism and Direct Experience:

31. Underhill, E. (1911/2002). Mysticism: A Study in the Nature and Development of Spiritual Consciousness. Dover Publications.

32. Stace, W.T. (1960). Mysticism and Philosophy. Macmillan.

33. Forman, R.K.C. (1999). Mysticism, Mind, Consciousness. SUNY Press.

34. Katz, S.T. (Ed.). (1978). Mysticism and Philosophical Analysis. Oxford University Press.

Contemporary Spiritual Teachers and Practitioners:

35. Dalai Lama. (1999). Ethics for the New Millennium. Riverhead Books.

36. Krishnamurti, J. (1969). Freedom from the Known. HarperOne.

37. Tolle, E. (1997). The Power of Now: A Guide to Spiritual Enlightenment. New World Library.

38. Thich Nhat Hanh. (1975). The Miracle of Mindfulness: An Introduction to the Practice of Meditation. Beacon Press.

Scientific and Philosophical Perspectives on Consciousness:

39. Chalmers, D. (1996). The Conscious Mind: In Search of a Fundamental Theory. Oxford University Press.

40. Dennett, D. (1991). Consciousness Explained. Little, Brown and Co.

41. Nagel, T. (1974). What Is It Like to Be a Bat? The Philosophical Review, 83(4), 435-450.

42. Damasio, A. (1999). The Feeling of What Happens: Body and Emotion in the Making of Consciousness. Harcourt Brace.

Ethics and Moral Philosophy:

43. Singer, P. (1979). Practical Ethics. Cambridge University Press.

44. MacIntyre, A. (1981). After Virtue: A Study in Moral Theory. University of Notre Dame Press.

45. Noddings, N. (1984). Caring: A Feminine Approach to Ethics and Moral Education. University of California Press.

Additional References

1. Vivekananda, S. (1896). Raja Yoga. Advaita Ashrama.

2. Aurobindo, S. (1940). The Life Divine. Sri Aurobindo Ashram.

3. Yogananda, P. (1946). Autobiography of a Yogi. Self-Realization Fellowship.

4. Krishnamurti, J. (1954). The First and Last Freedom. Harper & Brothers.

5. Easwaran, E. (translator). (2007). The Bhagavad Gita. Nilgiri Press.

6. Satchidananda, S. (translator). (1978). The Yoga Sutras of Patanjali. Integral Yoga Publications.

7. Nikhilananda, S. (translator). (1949). The Upanishads: A New Translation. Harper.

8. Vireswarananda, S. (translator). (1936). Brahma Sutras. Advaita Ashrama.

9. Madhavananda, S. (translator). (1921). Vivekachudamani of Sri Sankaracharya. Advaita Ashrama.

10. Radhakrishnan, S. (1927). The Hindu View of Life. Allen & Unwin.

11. Dasgupta, S. (1922). A History of Indian Philosophy. Cambridge University Press.

12. Coomaraswamy, A.K. (1947). Hinduism and Buddhism. Philosophical Library.

13. Chatterjee, S. & Datta, D. (1984). An Introduction to Indian Philosophy. University of Calcutta.

14. Sivananda, S. (1977). All About Hinduism. Divine Life Society.

15. Tolle, E. (1999). The Power of Now: A Guide to Spiritual Enlightenment. New World Library.

16. Adyashanti. (2008). The End of Your World: Uncensored Straight Talk on the Nature of Enlightenment. Sounds True.

17. Easwaran, E. (2007). The Upanishads (Classics of Indian Spirituality). Nilgiri Press.

18. Red Pine (translator). (2012). The Lankavatara Sutra: Translation and Commentary. Counterpoint.

19. Venkataramiah, M. (compiler). (2006). Talks with Sri Ramana Maharshi. Sri Ramanasramam.

20. Wilber, K. (2000). Integral Psychology: Consciousness, Spirit, Psychology, Therapy. Shambhala.

21. Goleman, D., & Davidson, R. J. (2017). Altered Traits: Science Reveals How Meditation Changes Your Mind, Brain, and Body. Avery.

22. Maharaj, N. (1973). I Am That: Talks with Sri Nisargadatta Maharaj. Acorn Press.

23. Huxley, A. (1945). The Perennial Philosophy. Harper & Brothers.

24. Suzuki, D.T. (1949). Essays in Zen Buddhism. Grove Press.

25. James, W. (1902). The Varieties of Religious Experience. Longmans, Green & Co.

26. Kornfield, J. (2000). After the Ecstasy, the Laundry: How the Heart Grows Wise on the Spiritual Path. Bantam.

27. Yogananda, P. (1946). Autobiography of a Yogi. Self-Realization Fellowship.

28. Watts, A. (1966). The Book: On the Taboo Against Knowing Who You Are. Vintage Books.

Chapter 5: Search for an easy path to true knowledge

Primary Texts and Translations:

1. Bhagavad Gita. (2007). (E. Easwaran, Trans.). Nilgiri Press.

2. The Upanishads. (2007). (E. Easwaran, Trans.). Nilgiri Press.

3. The Yoga Sutras of Patanjali. (1990). (C. Chapple & Y. Viraj, Trans.). Sri Satguru Publications.

4. Vivekachudamani of Adi Shankara. (1947). (Swami Madhavananda, Trans.). Advaita Ashrama.

5. Srimad Bhagavatam. (1976). (A.C. Bhaktivedanta Swami Prabhupada, Trans.). Bhaktivedanta Book Trust.

Classical Hindu Philosophy and Spirituality:

6. Radhakrishnan, S. (1953). The Principal Upanishads. Harper.

7. Dasgupta, S. (1922-1955). A History of Indian Philosophy (5 Volumes). Cambridge University Press.

8. Zimmer, H. (1951). Philosophies of India. Princeton University Press.

9. Aurobindo, S. (1999). The Synthesis of Yoga. Sri Aurobindo Ashram.

10. Vivekananda, S. (1907). Raja Yoga. Advaita Ashrama.

11. Yogananda, P. (1946). Autobiography of a Yogi. Self-Realization Fellowship.

Modern Interpretations and Commentaries:

12. Easwaran, E. (2007). The Bhagavad Gita for Daily Living (3 Volumes). Nilgiri Press.

13. Chinmayananda, S. (1992). The Holy Geeta. Central Chinmaya Mission Trust.

14. Maharshi, R. (1955). Talks with Sri Ramana Maharshi. Sri Ramanasramam.

15. Krishnamurti, J. (1954). The First and Last Freedom. Harper & Row.

16. Muktananda, S. (1978). Play of Consciousness. Harper & Row.

17. Sivananda, S. (1998). All About Hinduism. Divine Life Society.

Bhakti and Devotional Practices:

18. Bhaktivedanta Swami Prabhupada, A.C. (1970). The Nectar of Devotion. Bhaktivedanta Book Trust.

19. Ramakrishna. (1942). The Gospel of Sri Ramakrishna. (Swami Nikhilananda, Trans.). Ramakrishna-Vivekananda Center.

20. Tyagaraja. (2000). The Spiritual Heritage of Tyagaraja. (V. Raghavan, Trans.). Sri Ramakrishna Math.

Karma Yoga and Mindful Action:

21. Gandhi, M.K. (1946). The Gospel of Selfless Action or The Gita According to Gandhi. Navajivan Publishing House.

22. Vivekananda, S. (1896). Karma Yoga. Advaita Ashrama.

23. Chidbhavananda, S. (1997). The Bhagavad Gita: Commentary. Sri Ramakrishna Tapovanam.

Jnana Yoga and Self-Inquiry:

24. Nisargadatta Maharaj. (1973). I Am That. (M. Frydman, Trans.). Acorn Press.

25. Maharshi, R. (1997). Who Am I?: The Teachings of Bhagavan Sri Ramana Maharshi. Sri Ramanasramam.

26. Dayananda Saraswati, S. (2009). Introduction to Vedanta. Vision Books.

Mantra and Sound in Spiritual Practice:

27. Svoboda, R. (1993). Aghora II: Kundalini. Brotherhood of Life.

28. Ashley-Farrand, T. (1999). Healing Mantras. Ballantine Wellspring.

29. Kumar, R. (2009). The Power of Mantra and Mystery of Initiation. Lotus Press.

Yoga Philosophy and Practice:

30. Iyengar, B.K.S. (1966). Light on Yoga. Schocken Books.

31. Desikachar, T.K.V. (1995). The Heart of Yoga: Developing a Personal Practice. Inner Traditions.

32. Feuerstein, G. (1989). The Yoga-Sutra of Patanjali: A New Translation and Commentary. Inner Traditions.

Modern Spiritual Teachers and Practitioners:

33. Tolle, E. (1997). The Power of Now: A Guide to Spiritual Enlightenment. New World Library.

34. Dass, R. (1971). Be Here Now. Crown Publishing Group.

35. Mata Amritanandamayi. (1991). Awaken Children! (Vol. 1). M.A. Center.

36. Nithyananda, S. (2009). Living Enlightenment. Life Bliss Foundation.

Scholarly Works on Hindu Spirituality:

37. Flood, G. (1996). An Introduction to Hinduism. Cambridge University Press.

38. Klostermaier, K.K. (2007). A Survey of Hinduism. SUNY Press.

39. Eliade, M. (1958). Yoga: Immortality and Freedom. Princeton University Press.

40. Michaels, A. (2004). Hinduism: Past and Present. Princeton University Press.

Psychology and Hindu Spirituality:

41. Paranjpe, A.C. (1998). Self and Identity in Modern Psychology and Indian Thought. Springer.

42. Cornelissen, R.M.M., Misra, G., & Varma, S. (Eds.). (2011). Foundations of Indian Psychology. Pearson.

43. Rao, K.R., Paranjpe, A.C., & Dalal, A.K. (2008). Handbook of Indian Psychology. Cambridge University Press India.

Comparative Religion and Philosophy:

44. Smith, H. (1991). The World's Religions. HarperOne.

45. Huxley, A. (1945). The Perennial Philosophy. Harper & Brothers.

46. Wilber, K. (2000). Integral Psychology: Consciousness, Spirit, Psychology, Therapy. Shambhala.

Scientific Perspectives on Meditation and Spirituality:

47. Goleman, D., & Davidson, R.J. (2017). Altered Traits: Science Reveals How Meditation Changes Your Mind, Brain, and Body. Avery.

48. Wallace, B.A. (2007). Contemplative Science: Where Buddhism and Neuroscience Converge. Columbia University Press.

49. Hanson, R., & Mendius, R. (2009). Buddha's Brain: The Practical Neuroscience of Happiness, Love, and Wisdom. New Harbinger Publications.